4th Named Entity Workshop

(NEWS 2012)

Held at the 50th Annual Meeting of the Association for Computational Linguistics (ACL 2012)

Jeju, Republic of Korea
12 July 2012

ISBN: 978-1-62748-347-6

Printed from e-media with permission by:

Curran Associates, Inc.
57 Morehouse Lane
Red Hook, NY 12571

Some format issues inherent in the e-media version may also appear in this print version.

Printed by Curran Associates, Inc. (2013)

For permission requests, please contact the Association for Computational Linguistics at the address below.

Association for Computational Linguistics
209 N. Eighth Street
Stroudsburg, Pennsylvania 18360

Phone: 1-570-476-8006
Fax: 1-570-476-0860

acl@aclweb.org

Additional copies of this publication are available from:

Curran Associates, Inc.
57 Morehouse Lane
Red Hook, NY 12571 USA
Phone: 845-758-0400
Fax: 845-758-2634
Email: curran@proceedings.com
Web: www.proceedings.com

Preface

The workshop series, Named Entities WorkShop (NEWS), focuses on research on all aspects of the Named Entities, such as, identifying and analyzing named entities, mining, translating and transliterating named entities, etc. The first of the NEWS workshops (NEWS 2009) was held as a part of ACL-IJCNLP 2009 conference in Singapore; the second one, NEWS 2010, was held as an ACL 2010 workshop in Uppsala, Sweden; and the third one, NEWS 2011, was held as an IJCNLP 2011 workshop in Chiang Mai, Thailand. The current edition, NEWS 2012, was held as an ACL 2012 workshop in Jeju, Korea.

The purpose of the NEWS workshop series is to bring together researchers across the world interested in identification, analysis, extraction, mining and transformation of named entities in monolingual or multilingual natural language text corpora. The workshop scope includes many interesting specific research areas pertaining to the named entities, such as, orthographic and phonetic characteristics, corpus analysis, unsupervised and supervised named entities extraction in monolingual or multilingual corpus, transliteration modeling, and evaluation methodologies, to name a few. For this year edition, 7 research papers were submitted, each of which was reviewed by 3 reviewers from the program committee. 3 papers were chosen for publication, covering machine transliteration and transliteration mining from comparable corpus and wiki.

Following the tradition of the NEWS workshop series, NEWS 2012 continued the machine transliteration shared task this year as well. The shared task was first introduced in NEWS 2009 and continued in NEWS 2010 and NEWS 2011. In NEWS 2012, by leveraging on the previous success of NEWS workshop series, we released the hand-crafted parallel named entities corpora to include 14 different language pairs from 12 language families, and made them available as the common dataset for the shared task. In total, 7 international teams participated from around the globe. The approaches ranged from traditional learning methods (such as, Phrasal SMT-based, Conditional Random Fields, etc.) to somewhat new approaches (such as, RNN Language Model, Syllable-based Approach (Fine-grained English Segmentation), Two-Stage CRF, Optimization against multiple references and the intermediate representation of Chinese and Arabic). A report of the shared task that summarizes all submissions and the original whitepaper are also included in the proceedings, and will be presented in the workshop. The participants in the shared task were asked to submit short system papers (4 content pages each) describing their approaches, and each of such papers was reviewed by three members of the program committee to help improve the quality. All the 7 system papers were finally accepted to be published in the workshop proceedings.

We hope that NEWS 2012 would provide an exciting and productive forum for researchers working in this research area, and the NEWS-released data continues to serve as a standard dataset for machine transliteration generation and mining. We wish to thank all the researchers for their research submission and the enthusiastic participation in the transliteration shared tasks. We wish to express our gratitude to CJK Institute, Institute for Infocomm Research, Microsoft Research India, Thailand National Electronics and Computer Technology Centre and The Royal Melbourne Institute of Technology (RMIT)/Sarvnaz Karimi for preparing the data released as a part of the shared tasks. Finally, we thank all the program committee members for reviewing the submissions in spite of the tight schedule.

Workshop Chairs:
Min Zhang, Institute for Infocomm Research, Singapore
Haizhou Li, Institute for Infocomm Research, Singapore
A Kumaran, Microsoft Research, India

12 July 2012
Jeju, Korea

Organizers:

Workshop Co-Chair: Min Zhang, Institute for Infocomm Research, Singapore
Workshop Co-Chair: Haizhou Li, Institute for Infocomm Research, Singapore
Workshop Co-Chair: A Kumaran, Microsoft Research, India

Program Committee:

Kalika Bali, Microsoft Research, India
Rafael Banchs, Institute for Infocomm Research, Singapore
Sivaji Bandyopadhyay, University of Jadavpur, India
Pushpak Bhattacharyya, IIT-Bombay, India
Monojit Choudhury, Microsoft Research, India
Marta Ruiz Costa-jussa, UPC, Spain
Xiangyu Duan, Institute for Infocomm Research, Singapore
Gregory Grefenstette, Exalead, France
Guohong Fu, Heilongjiang University, China
Sarvnaz Karimi, NICTA and the University of Melbourne, Australia
Mitesh Khapra, IIT-Bombay, India
Greg Kondrak, University of Alberta, Canada
Olivia Kwong, City University, Hong Kong
Ming Liu, Institute for Infocomm Research, Singapore
Jong-Hoon Oh, NICT, Japan
Yan Qu, Advertising.com, USA
Keh-Yih Su, Behavior Design Corporation, Taiwan
Jun Sun, NUS, Singapore
Raghavendra Udupa, Microsoft Research, India
Vasudeva Varma, IIIT-Hyderabad, India
Haifeng Wang, Baidu.com, China
Chai Wutiwiwatchai, NECTEC, Thailand
Deyi Xiong, Institute for Infocomm Research, Singapore
Muyun Yang, HIT, China
Chengqing Zong, Institute of Automation, CAS, China

Table of Contents

Conference Program

Thursday, July 12, 2012

9:00–9:10 Opening Remarks by Min Zhang, Haizhou Li, A Kumaran and Ming Liu

Whitepaper of NEWS 2012 Shared Task on Machine Transliteration
Min Zhang, Haizhou Li, A Kumaran and Ming Liu

Report of NEWS 2012 Machine Transliteration Shared Task
Min Zhang, Haizhou Li, A Kumaran and Ming Liu

9:10–10:30 Session 1: Research Papers

09:10–09:35 *Accurate Unsupervised Joint Named-Entity Extraction from Unaligned Parallel Text*
Robert Munro and Christopher D. Manning

09:35–10:00 *Latent Semantic Transliteration using Dirichlet Mixture*
Masato Hagiwara and Satoshi Sekine

10:00–10:25 *Automatically generated NE tagged corpora for English and Hungarian*
Eszter Simon and Dávid Márk Nemeskey

10:30–11:00 Morning Break

11:00–12:30 Session 2: System Papers 1

11:00–11:25 *Rescoring a Phrase-based Machine Transliteration System with Recurrent Neural Network Language Models*
Andrew Finch, Paul Dixon and Eiichiro Sumita

11:25–11:50 *Syllable-based Machine Transliteration with Extra Phrase Features*
Chunyue Zhang, Tingting Li and Tiejun Zhao

11:50–12:15 *English-Korean Named Entity Transliteration Using Substring Alignment and Re-ranking Methods*
Chun-Kai Wu, Yu-Chun Wang and Richard Tzong-Han Tsai

12:15–13:45 Lunch Break

Thursday, July 12, 2012 (continued)

13:45–15:30 Session 3: System Papers 2

Whitepaper of NEWS 2012 Shared Task on Machine Transliteration*

Min Zhang†, Haizhou Li†, Ming Liu†, A Kumaran‡

†Institute for Infocomm Research, A*STAR, Singapore 138632
{mzhang,hli,mliu}@i2r.a-star.edu.sg

‡Multilingual Systems Research, Microsoft Research India
A.Kumaran@microsoft.com

Abstract

Transliteration is defined as phonetic translation of names across languages. Transliteration of Named Entities (NEs) is necessary in many applications, such as machine translation, corpus alignment, cross-language IR, information extraction and automatic lexicon acquisition. All such systems call for high-performance transliteration, which is the focus of shared task in the NEWS 2012 workshop. The objective of the shared task is to promote machine transliteration research by providing a common benchmarking platform for the community to evaluate the state-of-the-art technologies.

1 Task Description

The task is to develop machine transliteration system in one or more of the specified language pairs being considered for the task. Each language pair consists of a source and a target language. The training and development data sets released for each language pair are to be used for developing a transliteration system in whatever way that the participants find appropriate. At the evaluation time, a test set of source names only would be released, on which the participants are expected to produce a ranked list of transliteration candidates in another language (i.e. n-best transliterations), and this will be evaluated using common metrics. For every language pair the participants must submit at least one run that uses only the data provided by the NEWS workshop organisers in a given language pair (designated as "standard" run, primary submission). Users may submit more "stanrard" runs. They may also submit several "non-standard" runs for each language pair that use other data than those provided by the NEWS 2012 workshop; such runs would be evaluated and reported separately.

2 Important Dates

Research paper submission deadline	25 March 2012
Shared task	
Registration opens	18 Jan 2012
Registration closes	11 Mar 2012
Training/Development data release	20 Jan 2012
Test data release	12 Mar 2012
Results Submission Due	16 Mar 2012
Results Announcement	20 Mar 2012
Task (short) Papers Due	25 Mar 2012
For all submissions	
Acceptance Notification	20 April 2012
Camera-Ready Copy Deadline	30 April 2012
Workshop Date	12/13/14 July 2012

3 Participation

1. Registration (18 Jan 2012)
   (a) NEWS Shared Task opens for registration.
   (b) Prospective participants are to register to the NEWS Workshop homepage.

2. Training & Development Data (20 Jan 2012)
   (a) Registered participants are to obtain training and development data from the Shared Task organiser and/or the designated copyright owners of databases.
   (b) All registered participants are required to participate in the evaluation of at least one language pair, submit the results and a short paper and attend the workshop at ACL 2012.

3. Test data (12 March 2012)

*http://translit.i2r.a-star.edu.sg/news2012/

(a) The test data would be released on 12 March 2012, and the participants have a maximum of 5 days to submit their results in the expected format.

(b) One "standard" run must be submitted from every group on a given language pair. Additional "standard" runs may be submitted, up to 4 "standard" runs in total. However, the participants must indicate one of the submitted "standard" runs as the "primary submission". The primary submission will be used for the performance summary. In addition to the "standard" runs, more "non-standard" runs may be submitted. In total, maximum 8 runs (up to 4 "standard" runs plus up to 4 "non-standard" runs) can be submitted from each group on a registered language pair. The definition of "standard" and "non-standard" runs is in Section 5.

(c) Any runs that are "non-standard" must be tagged as such.

(d) The test set is a list of names in source language only. Every group will produce and submit a ranked list of transliteration candidates in another language for each given name in the test set. Please note that this shared task is a "transliteration generation" task, i.e., given a name in a source language one is supposed to generate one or more transliterations in a target language. It is not the task of "transliteration discovery", i.e., given a name in the source language and a set of names in the target language evaluate how to find the appropriate names from the target set that are transliterations of the given source name.

4. Results (20 March 2012)

(a) On 20 March 2012, the evaluation results would be announced and will be made available on the Workshop website.

(b) Note that only the scores (in respective metrics) of the participating systems on each language pairs would be published, and no explicit ranking of the participating systems would be published.

(c) Note that this is a shared evaluation task and not a competition; the results are meant to be used to evaluate systems on common data set with common metrics, and not to rank the participating systems. While the participants can cite the performance of their systems (scores on metrics) from the workshop report, they should not use any ranking information in their publications.

(d) Furthermore, all participants should agree not to reveal identities of other participants in any of their publications unless you get permission from the other respective participants. By default, all participants remain anonymous in published results, unless they indicate otherwise at the time of uploading their results. Note that the results of all systems will be published, but the identities of those participants that choose not to disclose their identity to other participants will be masked. As a result, in this case, your organisation name will still appear in the web site as one of participants, but it will not be linked explicitly to your results.

5. Short Papers on Task (25 March 2012)

(a) Each submitting site is required to submit a 4-page system paper (short paper) for its submissions, including their approach, data used and the results on either test set or development set or by n-fold cross validation on training set.

(b) The review of the system papers will be done to improve paper quality and readability and make sure the authors' ideas and methods can be understood by the workshop participants. We are aiming at accepting all system papers, and selected ones will be presented orally in the NEWS 2012 workshop.

(c) All registered participants are required to register and attend the workshop to introduce your work.

(d) All paper submission and review will be managed electronically through https://www.softconf.com/acl2012/news2012/.

4 Language Pairs

The tasks are to transliterate personal names or place names from a source to a target language as summarised in Table 1. NEWS 2012 Shared Task offers 14 evaluation subtasks, among them ChEn and ThEn are the back-transliteration of EnCh and EnTh tasks respectively. NEWS 2012 releases training, development and testing data for each of the language pairs. NEWS 2012 continues all language pairs that were evaluated in NEWS 2011. In such cases, the training and development data in the release of NEWS 2012 are the same as those in NEWS 2011. However, the test data in NEWS 2012 are entirely new.

Please note that in order to have an accurate study of the research progress of machine translation technology, different from previous practice, the test/reference sets of NEWS 2011 are not released to the research community. Instead, we use the test sets of NEWS 2011 as progress test sets in NEWS 2012. NEWS 2012 participants are requested to submit results on the NEWS 2012 progress test sets (i.e., NEWS 2011 test sets). By doing so, we would like to do comparison studies by comparing the NEWS 2012 and NEWS 2011 results on the progress test sets. We hope that we can have some insightful research findings in the progress studies.

The names given in the training sets for Chinese, Japanese, Korean, Thai and Persian languages are Western names and their respective transliterations; the Japanese Name (in English) → Japanese Kanji data set consists only of native Japanese names; the Arabic data set consists only of native Arabic names. The Indic data set (Hindi, Tamil, Kannada, Bangla) consists of a mix of Indian and Western names.

Examples of transliteration:

English → Chinese
Timothy → 蒂莫西

English → Japanese Katakana
Harrington → ハリントン

English → Korean Hangul
Bennett → 베넷

Japanese name in English → Japanese Kanji
Akihiro → 秋宏

English → Hindi
San Francisco → सैन फ्रान्सिस्को

English → Tamil
London → லண்டன்

English → Kannada
Tokyo → ಟೋಕ್ಯೋ

Arabic → Arabic name in English
خالد → Khalid

5 Standard Databases

Training Data (Parallel)
Paired names between source and target languages; size 7K – 37K.
Training Data is used for training a basic transliteration system.

Development Data (Parallel)
Paired names between source and target languages; size 1K – 2.8K.
Development Data is in addition to the Training data, which is used for system fine-tuning of parameters in case of need. Participants are allowed to use it as part of training data.

Testing Data
Source names only; size 1K – 2K.
This is a held-out set, which would be used for evaluating the quality of the transliterations.

Progress Testing Data
Source names only; size 0.6K – 2.6K.
This is the NEWS 2011 test set, it is held-out for progress study.

1. Participants will need to obtain licenses from the respective copyright owners and/or agree to the terms and conditions of use that are given on the downloading website (Li et al., 2004; MSRI, 2010; CJKI, 2010). NEWS 2011 will provide the contact details of each individual database. The data would be provided in Unicode UTF-8 encoding, in XML format; the results are expected to be submitted in UTF-8 encoding in XML format. The XML formats details are available in Appendix A.

2. The data are provided in 3 sets as described above.

3. Name pairs are distributed as-is, as provided by the respective creators.

Name origin	Source script	Target script	Data Owner	Data Size Train	Dev	Progress Test	2012 Test	Task ID
Western	English	Chinese	Institute for Infocomm Research	37K	2.8K	2K	1K	EnCh
Western	Chinese	English	Institute for Infocomm Research	28K	2.7K	2.2K	1K	ChEn
Western	English	Korean Hangul	CJK Institute	7K	1K	609	1K	EnKo
Western	English	Japanese Katakana	CJK Institute	26K	2K	1.8K	1K	EnJa
Japanese	English	Japanese Kanji	CJK Institute	10K	2K	571	1K	JnJk
Arabic	Arabic	English	CJK Institute	27K	2.5K	2.6K	1K	ArEn
Mixed	English	Hindi	Microsoft Research India	12K	1K	1K	1K	EnHi
Mixed	English	Tamil	Microsoft Research India	10K	1K	1K	1K	EnTa
Mixed	English	Kannada	Microsoft Research India	10K	1K	1K	1K	EnKa
Mixed	English	Bangla	Microsoft Research India	13K	1K	1K	1K	EnBa
Western	English	Thai	NECTEC	27K	2K	2K	1K	EnTh
Western	Thai	English	NECTEC	25K	2K	1.9K	1K	ThEn
Western	English	Persian	Sarvnaz Karimi / RMIT	10K	2K	2K	1K	EnPe
Western	English	Hebrew	Microsoft Research India	9.5K	1K	1K	1K	EnHe

Table 1: Source and target languages for the shared task on transliteration.

   (a) While the databases are mostly manually checked, there may be still inconsistency (that is, non-standard usage, region-specific usage, errors, etc.) or incompleteness (that is, not all right variations may be covered).
   (b) The participants may use any method to further clean up the data provided.
      i. If they are cleaned up manually, we appeal that such data be provided back to the organisers for redistribution to all the participating groups in that language pair; such sharing benefits all participants, and further ensures that the evaluation provides normalisation with respect to data quality.
      ii. If automatic cleanup were used, such cleanup would be considered a part of the system fielded, and hence not required to be shared with all participants.

4. *Standard Runs* We expect that the participants to use only the data (parallel names) provided by the Shared Task for transliteration task for a "standard" run to ensure a fair evaluation. One such run (using only the data provided by the shared task) is mandatory for all participants for a given language pair that they participate in.

5. *Non-standard Runs* If more data (either parallel names data or monolingual data) were used, then all such runs using extra data must be marked as "non-standard". For such "non-standard" runs, it is required to disclose the size and characteristics of the data used in the system paper.

6. A participant may submit a maximum of 8 runs for a given language pair (including the mandatory 1 "standard" run marked as "primary submission").

6 Paper Format

Paper submissions to NEWS 2012 should follow the ACL 2012 paper submission policy, including paper format, blind review policy and title and author format convention. Full papers (research paper) are in two-column format without exceeding eight (8) pages of content plus two (2) extra page for references and short papers (task paper) are also in two-column format without exceeding four (4) pages content plus two (2) extra page for references. Submission must conform to the official ACL 2012 style guidelines. For details, please refer to the ACL 2012 website[2].

7 Evaluation Metrics

We plan to measure the quality of the transliteration task using the following 4 metrics. We accept up to 10 output candidates in a ranked list for each input entry.

Since a given source name may have multiple correct target transliterations, all these alternatives are treated equally in the evaluation. That is, any of these alternatives are considered as a correct transliteration, and the first correct transliteration in the ranked list is accepted as a correct hit.

[2]http://www.ACL2012.org/

The following notation is further assumed:

N : Total number of names (source words) in the test set

n_i : Number of reference transliterations for i-th name in the test set ($n_i \geq 1$)

$r_{i,j}$: j-th reference transliteration for i-th name in the test set

$c_{i,k}$: k-th candidate transliteration (system output) for i-th name in the test set ($1 \leq k \leq 10$)

K_i : Number of candidate transliterations produced by a transliteration system

1. Word Accuracy in Top-1 (ACC) Also known as Word Error Rate, it measures correctness of the first transliteration candidate in the candidate list produced by a transliteration system. $ACC = 1$ means that all top candidates are correct transliterations i.e. they match one of the references, and $ACC = 0$ means that none of the top candidates are correct.

$$ACC = \frac{1}{N}\sum_{i=1}^{N}\left\{ \begin{array}{l} 1 \text{ if } \exists\, r_{i,j} : r_{i,j} = c_{i,1}; \\ 0 \text{ otherwise} \end{array} \right\} \quad (1)$$

2. Fuzziness in Top-1 (Mean F-score) The mean F-score measures how different, on average, the top transliteration candidate is from its closest reference. F-score for each source word is a function of Precision and Recall and equals 1 when the top candidate matches one of the references, and 0 when there are no common characters between the candidate and any of the references.

Precision and Recall are calculated based on the length of the Longest Common Subsequence between a candidate and a reference:

$$LCS(c,r) = \frac{1}{2}\left(|c| + |r| - ED(c,r)\right) \quad (2)$$

where ED is the edit distance and $|x|$ is the length of x. For example, the longest common subsequence between "abcd" and "afcde" is "acd" and its length is 3. The best matching reference, that is, the reference for which the edit distance has the minimum, is taken for calculation. If the best matching reference is given by

$$r_{i,m} = \arg\min_{j}\left(ED(c_{i,1}, r_{i,j})\right) \quad (3)$$

then Recall, Precision and F-score for i-th word are calculated as

$$R_i = \frac{LCS(c_{i,1}, r_{i,m})}{|r_{i,m}|} \quad (4)$$

$$P_i = \frac{LCS(c_{i,1}, r_{i,m})}{|c_{i,1}|} \quad (5)$$

$$F_i = 2\frac{R_i \times P_i}{R_i + P_i} \quad (6)$$

- The length is computed in distinct Unicode characters.
- No distinction is made on different character types of a language (e.g., vowel vs. consonants vs. combining diereses' etc.)

3. Mean Reciprocal Rank (MRR) Measures traditional MRR *for any right answer* produced by the system, from among the candidates. $1/MRR$ tells approximately the average rank of the correct transliteration. MRR closer to 1 implies that the correct answer is mostly produced close to the top of the n-best lists.

$$RR_i = \left\{ \begin{array}{l} \min_j \frac{1}{j} \text{ if } \exists r_{i,j}, c_{i,k} : r_{i,j} = c_{i,k}; \\ 0 \text{ otherwise} \end{array} \right\} \quad (7)$$

$$MRR = \frac{1}{N}\sum_{i=1}^{N} RR_i \quad (8)$$

4. MAP$_{ref}$ Measures tightly the precision in the n-best candidates for i-th source name, for which reference transliterations are available. If all of the references are produced, then the MAP is 1. Let's denote the number of correct candidates for the i-th source word in k-best list as $num(i,k)$. MAP$_{ref}$ is then given by

$$MAP_{ref} = \frac{1}{N}\sum_{i}^{N}\frac{1}{n_i}\left(\sum_{k=1}^{n_i} num(i,k)\right) \quad (9)$$

8 Contact Us

If you have any questions about this share task and the database, please email to

Mr. Ming Liu

Institute for Infocomm Research (I^{2}R), A*STAR

1 Fusionopolis Way

#08-05 South Tower, Connexis

Singapore 138632

mliu@i2r.a-star.edu.sg

Dr. Min Zhang
Institute for Infocomm Research (I^2R), A*STAR
1 Fusionopolis Way
#08-05 South Tower, Connexis
Singapore 138632
mzhang@i2r.a-star.edu.sg

References

[CJKI2010] CJKI. 2010. CJK Institute. http://www.cjk.org/.

[Li et al.2004] Haizhou Li, Min Zhang, and Jian Su. 2004. A joint source-channel model for machine transliteration. In *Proc. 42nd ACL Annual Meeting*, pages 159–166, Barcelona, Spain.

[MSRI2010] MSRI. 2010. Microsoft Research India. http://research.microsoft.com/india.

A Training/Development Data

- File Naming Conventions:
  NEWS12_train_XXYY_nnnn.xml
  NEWS12_dev_XXYY_nnnn.xml
  NEWS12_test_XXYY_nnnn.xml
  NEWS11_test_XXYY_nnnn.xml
  (progress test sets)
  - XX: Source Language
  - YY: Target Language
  - nnnn: size of parallel/monolingual names ("25K", "10000", etc)
- File formats:
  All data will be made available in XML formats (Figure 1).
- Data Encoding Formats:
  The data will be in Unicode UTF-8 encoding files without byte-order mark, and in the XML format specified.

B Submission of Results

- File Naming Conventions:
  You can give your files any name you like. During submission online you will need to indicate whether this submission belongs to a "standard" or "non-standard" run, and if it is a "standard" run, whether it is the primary submission.
- File formats:
  All data will be made available in XML formats (Figure 2).
- Data Encoding Formats:
  The results are expected to be submitted in UTF-8 encoded files without byte-order mark only, and in the XML format specified.

```
<?xml version="1.0" encoding="UTF-8"?>

<TransliterationCorpus
    CorpusID = "NEWS2012-Train-EnHi-25K"
    SourceLang = "English"
    TargetLang = "Hindi"
    CorpusType = "Train|Dev"
    CorpusSize = "25000"
    CorpusFormat = "UTF8">

    <Name ID=" 1" >
        <SourceName>eeeeee1</SourceName>
        <TargetName ID="1">hhhhhh1_1</TargetName>
            <TargetName ID="2">hhhhhh1_2</TargetName>
        ...
        <TargetName ID="n">hhhhhh1_n</TargetName>
    </Name>
    <Name ID=" 2" >
        <SourceName>eeeeee2</SourceName>
        <TargetName ID="1">hhhhhh2_1</TargetName>
        <TargetName ID="2">hhhhhh2_2</TargetName>
        ...
        <TargetName ID="m">hhhhhh2_m</TargetName>
    </Name>
    ...
    <!-- rest of the names to follow -->
    ...
</TransliterationCorpus>
```

Figure 1: File: NEWS2012_Train_EnHi_25K.xml

```xml
<?xml version="1.0" encoding="UTF-8"?>

<TransliterationTaskResults
    SourceLang = "English"
    TargetLang = "Hindi"
    GroupID = "Trans University"
    RunID = "1"
    RunType = "Standard"
    Comments = "HMM Run with params: alpha=0.8 beta=1.25">

    <Name ID="1">
        <SourceName>eeeeee1</SourceName>
        <TargetName ID="1">hhhhhh11</TargetName>
        <TargetName ID="2">hhhhhh12</TargetName>
        <TargetName ID="3">hhhhhh13</TargetName>
        ...
        <TargetName ID="10">hhhhhh110</TargetName>

        <!-- Participants to provide their
        top 10 candidate transliterations -->
    </Name>
    <Name ID="2">
        <SourceName>eeeeee2</SourceName>
        <TargetName ID="1">hhhhhh21</TargetName>
        <TargetName ID="2">hhhhhh22</TargetName>
        <TargetName ID="3">hhhhhh23</TargetName>
        ...
        <TargetName ID="10">hhhhhh110</TargetName>
        <!-- Participants to provide their
        top 10 candidate transliterations -->
    </Name>
    ...
    <!-- All names in test corpus to follow -->
    ...
</TransliterationTaskResults>
```

Figure 2: Example file: NEWS2012_EnHi_TUniv_01_StdRunHMMBased.xml

Report of NEWS 2012 Machine Transliteration Shared Task

Min Zhang[†], Haizhou Li[†], A Kumaran[‡] and Ming Liu [†]

[†]Institute for Infocomm Research, A*STAR, Singapore 138632
{mzhang,hli,mliu}@i2r.a-star.edu.sg

[‡]Multilingual Systems Research, Microsoft Research India
A.Kumaran@microsoft.com

Abstract

This report documents the Machine Transliteration Shared Task conducted as a part of the Named Entities Workshop (NEWS 2012), an ACL 2012 workshop. The shared task features machine transliteration of proper names from English to 11 languages and from 3 languages to English. In total, 14 tasks are provided. 7 teams participated in the evaluations. Finally, 57 standard and 1 non-standard runs are submitted, where diverse transliteration methodologies are explored and reported on the evaluation data. We report the results with 4 performance metrics. We believe that the shared task has successfully achieved its objective by providing a common benchmarking platform for the research community to evaluate the state-of-the-art technologies that benefit the future research and development.

1 Introduction

Names play a significant role in many Natural Language Processing (NLP) and Information Retrieval (IR) systems. They are important in Cross Lingual Information Retrieval (CLIR) and Machine Translation (MT) as the system performance has been shown to positively correlate with the correct conversion of names between the languages in several studies (Demner-Fushman and Oard, 2002; Mandl and Womser-Hacker, 2005; Hermjakob et al., 2008; Udupa et al., 2009). The traditional source for name equivalence, the bilingual dictionaries — whether handcrafted or statistical — offer only limited support because new names always emerge.

All of the above point to the critical need for robust Machine Transliteration technology and systems. Much research effort has been made to address the transliteration issue in the research community (Knight and Graehl, 1998; Meng et al., 2001; Li et al., 2004; Zelenko and Aone, 2006; Sproat et al., 2006; Sherif and Kondrak, 2007; Hermjakob et al., 2008; Al-Onaizan and Knight, 2002; Goldwasser and Roth, 2008; Goldberg and Elhadad, 2008; Klementiev and Roth, 2006; Oh and Choi, 2002; Virga and Khudanpur, 2003; Wan and Verspoor, 1998; Kang and Choi, 2000; Gao et al., 2004; Zelenko and Aone, 2006; Li et al., 2009b; Li et al., 2009a). These previous work fall into three categories, i.e., grapheme-based, phoneme-based and hybrid methods. Grapheme-based method (Li et al., 2004) treats transliteration as a direct orthographic mapping and only uses orthography-related features while phoneme-based method (Knight and Graehl, 1998) makes use of phonetic correspondence to generate the transliteration. Hybrid method refers to the combination of several different models or knowledge sources to support the transliteration generation.

The first machine transliteration shared task (Li et al., 2009b; Li et al., 2009a) was held in NEWS 2009 at ACL-IJCNLP 2009. It was the first time to provide common benchmarking data in diverse language pairs for evaluation of state-of-the-art techniques. While the focus of the 2009 shared task was on establishing the quality metrics and on baselining the transliteration quality based on those metrics, the 2010 shared task (Li et al., 2010a; Li et al., 2010b) expanded the scope of the transliteration generation task to about a dozen languages, and explored the quality depending on the direction of transliteration, between the languages. In NEWS 2011 (Zhang et al., 2011a; Zhang et al., 2011b), we significantly increased the hand-crafted parallel named entities corpora to include 14 different language pairs from 11 language families, and made them available as the common dataset for the shared task. NEWS 2012 was a continued effort of NEWS 2011, NEWS

2010 and NEWS 2009.

The rest of the report is organised as follows. Section 2 outlines the machine transliteration task and the corpora used and Section 3 discusses the metrics chosen for evaluation, along with the rationale for choosing them. Sections 4 and 5 present the participation in the shared task and the results with their analysis, respectively. Section 6 concludes the report.

2 Transliteration Shared Task

In this section, we outline the definition and the description of the shared task.

2.1 "Transliteration": A definition

There exists several terms that are used interchangeably in the contemporary research literature for the conversion of names between two languages, such as, transliteration, transcription, and sometimes Romanisation, especially if Latin scripts are used for target strings (Halpern, 2007).

Our aim is not only at capturing the name conversion process from a source to a target language, but also at its practical utility for downstream applications, such as CLIR and MT. Therefore, we adopted the same definition of transliteration as during the NEWS 2009 workshop (Li et al., 2009a) to narrow down "transliteration" to three specific requirements for the task, as follows: *"Transliteration is the conversion of a given name in the source language (a text string in the source writing system or orthography) to a name in the target language (another text string in the target writing system or orthography), such that the target language name is: (i) phonemically equivalent to the source name (ii) conforms to the phonology of the target language and (iii) matches the user intuition of the equivalent of the source language name in the target language, considering the culture and orthographic character usage in the target language."*

Following NEWS 2011, in NEWS 2012, we still keep the three back-transliteration tasks. We define back-transliteration as a process of restoring transliterated words to their original languages. For example, NEWS 2012 offers the tasks to convert western names written in Chinese and Thai into their original English spellings, and romanized Japanese names into their original Kanji writings.

2.2 Shared Task Description

Following the tradition of NEWS workshop series, the shared task at NEWS 2012 is specified as development of machine transliteration systems in one or more of the specified language pairs. Each language pair of the shared task consists of a source and a target language, implicitly specifying the transliteration direction. Training and development data in each of the language pairs have been made available to all registered participants for developing a transliteration system for that specific language pair using any approach that they find appropriate.

At the evaluation time, a standard hand-crafted test set consisting of between 500 and 3,000 source names (approximately 5-10% of the training data size) have been released, on which the participants are required to produce a ranked list of transliteration candidates in the target language for each source name. The system output is tested against a reference set (which may include multiple correct transliterations for some source names), and the performance of a system is captured in multiple metrics (defined in Section 3), each designed to capture a specific performance dimension.

For every language pair each participant is required to submit at least one run (designated as a "standard" run) that uses only the data provided by the NEWS workshop organisers in that language pair, and no other data or linguistic resources. This standard run ensures parity between systems and enables meaningful comparison of performance of various algorithmic approaches in a given language pair. Participants are allowed to submit more "standard" runs, up to 4 in total. If more than one "standard" runs is submitted, it is required to name one of them as a "primary" run, which is used to compare results across different systems. In addition, up to 4 "non-standard" runs could be submitted for every language pair using either data beyond that provided by the shared task organisers or linguistic resources in a specific language, or both. This essentially may enable any participant to demonstrate the limits of performance of their system in a given language pair.

The shared task timelines provide adequate time for development, testing (more than 1 month after the release of the training data) and the final result submission (4 days after the release of the test data).

2.3 Shared Task Corpora

We considered two specific constraints in selecting languages for the shared task: language diversity and data availability. To make the shared task interesting and to attract wider participation, it is important to ensure a reasonable variety among the languages in terms of linguistic diversity, orthography and geography. Clearly, the ability of procuring and distributing a reasonably large (approximately 10K paired names for training and testing together) hand-crafted corpora consisting primarily of paired names is critical for this process. At the end of the planning stage and after discussion with the data providers, we have chosen the set of 14 tasks shown in Table 1 (Li et al., 2004; Kumaran and Kellner, 2007; MSRI, 2009; CJKI, 2010).

NEWS 2012 leverages on the success of NEWS 2011 by utilizing the training set of NEWS 2011 as the training data of NEWS 2012 and the dev data of NEWS 2011 as the dev data of NEWS 2012. NEWS 2012 provides entirely new test data across all 14 tasks for evaluation.

The names given in the training sets for Chinese, Japanese, Korean, Thai, Persian and Hebrew languages are Western names and their respective transliterations; the Japanese Name (in English) → Japanese Kanji data set consists only of native Japanese names; the Arabic data set consists only of native Arabic names. The Indic data set (Hindi, Tamil, Kannada, Bangla) consists of a mix of Indian and Western names.

For all of the tasks chosen, we have been able to procure paired names data between the source and the target scripts and were able to make them available to the participants. For some language pairs, such as English-Chinese and English-Thai, there are both transliteration and back-transliteration tasks. Most of the task are just one-way transliteration, although Indian data sets contained mixture of names of both Indian and Western origins. The language of origin of the names for each task is indicated in the first column of Table 1.

Finally, it should be noted here that the corpora procured and released for NEWS 2012 represent perhaps the most diverse and largest corpora to be used for any common transliteration tasks today.

3 Evaluation Metrics and Rationale

The participants have been asked to submit results of up to four standard and four non-standard runs. One standard run must be named as the primary submission and is used for the performance summary. Each run contains a ranked list of up to 10 candidate transliterations for each source name. The submitted results are compared to the ground truth (reference transliterations) using 4 evaluation metrics capturing different aspects of transliteration performance. The same as the NEWS 2011, we have dropped two MAP metrics used in NEWS 2009 because they don't offer additional information to MAP_{ref}. Since a name may have multiple correct transliterations, all these alternatives are treated equally in the evaluation, that is, any of these alternatives is considered as a correct transliteration, and all candidates matching any of the reference transliterations are accepted as correct ones.

The following notation is further assumed:

- N : Total number of names (source words) in the test set
- n_i : Number of reference transliterations for i-th name in the test set ($n_i \geq 1$)
- $r_{i,j}$: j-th reference transliteration for i-th name in the test set
- $c_{i,k}$: k-th candidate transliteration (system output) for i-th name in the test set ($1 \leq k \leq 10$)
- K_i : Number of candidate transliterations produced by a transliteration system

3.1 Word Accuracy in Top-1 (ACC)

Also known as Word Error Rate, it measures correctness of the first transliteration candidate in the candidate list produced by a transliteration system. $ACC = 1$ means that all top candidates are correct transliterations i.e. they match one of the references, and $ACC = 0$ means that none of the top candidates are correct.

$$ACC = \frac{1}{N}\sum_{i=1}^{N}\left\{\begin{array}{l} 1 \text{ if } \exists r_{i,j} : r_{i,j} = c_{i,1}; \\ 0 \text{ otherwise} \end{array}\right\} \quad (1)$$

3.2 Fuzziness in Top-1 (Mean F-score)

The mean F-score measures how different, on average, the top transliteration candidate is from its closest reference. F-score for each source word

Name origin	Source script	Target script	Data Owner	Data Size			Task ID	
				Train	Dev	Test		
Western	English	Chinese	Institute for Infocomm Research	37K	2.8K	2K	1K	EnCh
Western	Chinese	English	Institute for Infocomm Research	28K	2.7K	2.2K	1K	ChEn
Western	English	Korean Hangul	CJK Institute	7K	1K	609	1K	EnKo
Western	English	Japanese Katakana	CJK Institute	26K	2K	1.8K	1K	EnJa
Japanese	English	Japanese Kanji	CJK Institute	10K	2K	571	1K	JnJk
Arabic	Arabic	English	CJK Institute	27K	2.5K	2.6K	1K	ArEn
Mixed	English	Hindi	Microsoft Research India	12K	1K	1K	1K	EnHi
Mixed	English	Tamil	Microsoft Research India	10K	1K	1K	1K	EnTa
Mixed	English	Kannada	Microsoft Research India	10K	1K	1K	1K	EnKa
Mixed	English	Bangla	Microsoft Research India	13K	1K	1K	1K	EnBa
Western	English	Thai	NECTEC	27K	2K	2K	1K	EnTh
Western	Thai	English	NECTEC	25K	2K	1.9K	1K	ThEn
Western	English	Persian	Sarvnaz Karimi / RMIT	10K	2K	2K	1K	EnPe
Western	English	Hebrew	Microsoft Research India	9.5K	1K	1K	1K	EnHe

Table 1: Source and target languages for the shared task on transliteration.

is a function of Precision and Recall and equals 1 when the top candidate matches one of the references, and 0 when there are no common characters between the candidate and any of the references.

Precision and Recall are calculated based on the length of the Longest Common Subsequence (LCS) between a candidate and a reference:

$$LCS(c, r) = \frac{1}{2}\left(|c| + |r| - ED(c, r)\right) \quad (2)$$

where ED is the edit distance and $|x|$ is the length of x. For example, the longest common subsequence between "abcd" and "afcde" is "acd" and its length is 3. The best matching reference, that is, the reference for which the edit distance has the minimum, is taken for calculation. If the best matching reference is given by

$$r_{i,m} = \arg\min_j \left(ED(c_{i,1}, r_{i,j})\right) \quad (3)$$

then Recall, Precision and F-score for i-th word are calculated as

$$R_i = \frac{LCS(c_{i,1}, r_{i,m})}{|r_{i,m}|} \quad (4)$$

$$P_i = \frac{LCS(c_{i,1}, r_{i,m})}{|c_{i,1}|} \quad (5)$$

$$F_i = 2\frac{R_i \times P_i}{R_i + P_i} \quad (6)$$

- The length is computed in distinct Unicode characters.
- No distinction is made on different character types of a language (e.g., vowel vs. consonants vs. combining diereses etc.)

3.3 Mean Reciprocal Rank (MRR)

Measures traditional MRR *for any right answer* produced by the system, from among the candidates. $1/MRR$ tells approximately the average rank of the correct transliteration. MRR closer to 1 implies that the correct answer is mostly produced close to the top of the n-best lists.

$$RR_i = \left\{ \begin{array}{l} \min_j \frac{1}{j} \text{ if } \exists r_{i,j}, c_{i,k} : r_{i,j} = c_{i,k}; \\ 0 \text{ otherwise} \end{array} \right\} \quad (7)$$

$$MRR = \frac{1}{N}\sum_{i=1}^{N} RR_i \quad (8)$$

3.4 MAP$_{ref}$

Measures tightly the precision in the n-best candidates for i-th source name, for which reference transliterations are available. If all of the references are produced, then the MAP is 1. Let's denote the number of correct candidates for the i-th source word in k-best list as $num(i, k)$. MAP$_{ref}$ is then given by

$$MAP_{ref} = \frac{1}{N}\sum_{i}^{N}\frac{1}{n_i}\left(\sum_{k=1}^{n_i} num(i, k)\right) \quad (9)$$

4 Participation in Shared Task

7 teams submitted their transliteration results. Table 3 shows the details of registration tasks. Teams are required to submit at least one standard run for every task they participated in. In total, we receive 57 standard and 1 non-standard runs. Table 2 shows the number of standard and non-standard runs submitted for each task. It is clear that the most "popular" task is the transliteration from English to Chinese being attempted by 7 participants.

	English to Chinese	Chinese to English	English to Thai	Thai to English	English to Hindi	English to Tamil	English to Kannada
Language pair code	EnCh	ChEn	EnTh	ThEn	EnHi	EnTa	EnKa
Standard runs	14	5	2	2	2	2	2
Non-standard runs	0	0	0	0	0	0	0

	English to Japanese Katakana	English to Korean Hangul	English to Japanese Kanji	Arabic to English	English to Bengali (Bangla)	English to Persian	English to Hebrew
Language pair code	EnJa	EnKo	JnJk	ArEn	EnBa	EnPe	EnHe
Standard runs	3	4	4	5	4	4	4
Non-standard runs	0	1	0	0	0	0	0

Table 2: Number of runs submitted for each task. Number of participants coincides with the number of standard runs submitted.

Team ID	Organisation	EnCh	ChEn	EnTh	ThEn	EnHi	EnTa	EnKa	EnJa	EnKo	JnJk	ArEn	EnBa	EnPe	EnHe
1	University of Alberta											x			
2	NICT	x	x	x	x	x	x	x	x	x	x	x	x	x	x
3	MIT@Lab of HIT		x												
4	IASL, Academia Sinica	x													
5	Yahoo Japan Corporation	x	x						x	x	x		x	x	x
6	Yuan Ze University									x					
7	CMU	x	x	x	x	x	x	x	x	x	x	x	x	x	x

Table 3: Participation of teams in different tasks.

5 Task Results and Analysis

5.1 Standard runs

All the results are presented numerically in Tables 4–17, for all evaluation metrics. These are the official evaluation results published for this edition of the transliteration shared task.

The methodologies used in the ten submitted system papers are summarized as follows. Similar to their NEWS 2011 system, Finch et al. (2012) employ non-Parametric Bayesian method to co-segment bilingual named entities for model training and report very good performance. This system is based on phrase-based statistical machine transliteration (SMT) (Finch and Sumita, 2008), an approach initially developed for machine translation (Koehn et al., 2003), where the SMT system's log-linear model is augmented with a set of features specifically suited to the task of transliteration. In particular, the model utilizes a feature based on a joint source-channel model, and a feature based on a maximum entropy model that predicts target grapheme sequences using the local context of graphemes and grapheme sequences in both source and target languages. Different from their NEWS 2011 system, in order to solve the data sparseness issue, they use two RNN-based LM to project the grapheme set onto a smaller hidden representation: one for the target grapheme sequence and the other for the sequence of grapheme sequence pair used to generate the target.

Zhang et al. (2012) also use the statistical phrase-based SMT framework. They propose the fine-grained English segmentation algorithm and other new features and achieve very good performance. Wu et al. (2012) uses m2m-aligner and DirecTL-p decoder and two re-ranking methods: co-occurrence at web corpus and JLIS-Reranking method based on the features from alignment results. They report very good performance at English-Korean tasks. Okuno (2012) studies the mpaligner (an improvement of m2m-aligner) and shows that mpaligner is more effective than m2m-aligner. They also find that de-romanization is crucial to JnJk task and mora is the best alignment unit for EnJa task. Ammar et al. (2012) use CRF as the basic model but with two innovations: a training objective that optimizes toward any of a set of possible correct labels (i.e., multiple references) and a k-best reranking with non-local features. Their results on ArEn show that the two features are very effective in accuracy improvement. Kondrak et al. (2012) study the language-specific adaptations in the context of two language pairs: English to Chinese (Pinyin representation) and Arabic to English (letter mapping). They conclude that Pinyin representation is useful while letter mapping is less effective. Kuo et al. (2012) explore two-stage CRF for Enligsh-to-Chinese task and show that the two-stage CRF outperform traditional one-stage CRF.

5.2 Non-standard runs

For the non-standard runs, we pose no restrictions on the use of data or other linguistic resources. The purpose of non-standard runs is to see how best personal name transliteration can be, for a given language pair. In NEWS 2012, only one non-standard run (Wu et al., 2012) was submitted. Their reported web-based re-validation method is very effective.

6 Conclusions and Future Plans

The Machine Transliteration Shared Task in NEWS 2012 shows that the community has a continued interest in this area. This report summarizes the results of the shared task. Again, we are pleased to report a comprehensive calibration and baselining of machine transliteration approaches as most state-of-the-art machine transliteration techniques are represented in the shared task.

In addition to the most popular techniques such as Phrase-Based Machine Transliteration (Koehn et al., 2003), CRF, re-ranking, DirecTL-p decoder, Non-Parametric Bayesian Co-segmentation (Finch et al., 2011), and Multi-to-Multi Joint Source Channel Model (Chen et al., 2011) in the NEWS 2011, we are delighted to see that several new techniques have been proposed and explored with promising results reported, including RNN-based LM (Finch et al., 2012), English Segmentation algorithm (Zhang et al., 2012), JLIS-reranking method (Wu et al., 2012), improved m2m-aligner (Okuno, 2012), multiple reference-optimized CRF (Ammar et al., 2012), language dependent adaptation (Kondrak et al., 2012) and two-stage CRF (Kuo et al., 2012). As the standard runs are limited by the use of corpus, most of the systems are implemented under the direct orthographic mapping (DOM) framework (Li et al., 2004). While the standard runs allow us to conduct meaningful comparison across different algorithms, we recognise that the non-standard runs open up more opportunities for exploiting a variety of additional linguistic corpora.

Encouraged by the success of the NEWS workshop series, we would like to continue this event in the future conference to promote the machine transliteration research and development.

Acknowledgements

The organisers of the NEWS 2012 Shared Task would like to thank the Institute for Infocomm Research (Singapore), Microsoft Research India, CJK Institute (Japan), National Electronics and Computer Technology Center (Thailand) and Sarvnaz Karim / RMIT for providing the corpora and technical support. Without those, the Shared Task would not be possible. We thank those participants who identified errors in the data and sent us the errata. We also want to thank the members of programme committee for their invaluable comments that improve the quality of the shared task papers. Finally, we wish to thank all the participants for their active participation that have made this first machine transliteration shared task a comprehensive one.

References

Yaser Al-Onaizan and Kevin Knight. 2002. Machine transliteration of names in arabic text. In *Proc. ACL-2002 Workshop: Computational Apporaches to Semitic Languages*, Philadelphia, PA, USA.

Waleed Ammar, Chris Dyer, and Noah Smith. 2012. Transliteration by sequence labeling with lattice encodings and reranking. In *Proc. Named Entities Workshop at ACL 2012*.

Yu Chen, Rui Wang, and Yi Zhang. 2011. Statistical machine transliteration with multi-to-multi joint source channel model. In *Proc. Named Entities Workshop at IJCNLP 2011*.

CJKI. 2010. CJK Institute. http://www.cjk.org/.

D. Demner-Fushman and D. W. Oard. 2002. The effect of bilingual term list size on dictionary-based cross-language information retrieval. In *Proc. 36-th Hawaii Int'l. Conf. System Sciences*, volume 4, page 108.2.

Andrew Finch and Eiichiro Sumita. 2008. Phrase-based machine transliteration. In *Proc. 3rd Int'l. Joint Conf NLP*, volume 1, Hyderabad, India, January.

Andrew Finch, Paul Dixon, and Eiichiro Sumita. 2011. Integrating models derived from non-parametric bayesian co-segmentation into a statistical machine transliteration system. In *Proc. Named Entities Workshop at IJCNLP 2011*.

Andrew Finch, Paul Dixon, and Eiichiro Sumita. 2012. Rescoring a phrase-based machine transliteration system with recurrent neural network language models. In *Proc. Named Entities Workshop at ACL 2012*.

Wei Gao, Kam-Fai Wong, and Wai Lam. 2004. Phoneme-based transliteration of foreign names for OOV problem. In *Proc. IJCNLP*, pages 374–381, Sanya, Hainan, China.

Yoav Goldberg and Michael Elhadad. 2008. Identification of transliterated foreign words in Hebrew script. In *Proc. CICLing*, volume LNCS 4919, pages 466–477.

Dan Goldwasser and Dan Roth. 2008. Transliteration as constrained optimization. In *Proc. EMNLP*, pages 353–362.

Jack Halpern. 2007. The challenges and pitfalls of Arabic romanization and arabization. In *Proc. Workshop on Comp. Approaches to Arabic Script-based Lang.*

Ulf Hermjakob, Kevin Knight, and Hal Daumé. 2008. Name translation in statistical machine translation: Learning when to transliterate. In *Proc. ACL*, Columbus, OH, USA, June.

Byung-Ju Kang and Key-Sun Choi. 2000. English-Korean automatic transliteration/back-transliteration system and character alignment. In *Proc. ACL*, pages 17–18, Hong Kong.

Alexandre Klementiev and Dan Roth. 2006. Weakly supervised named entity transliteration and discovery from multilingual comparable corpora. In *Proc. 21st Int'l Conf Computational Linguistics and 44th Annual Meeting of ACL*, pages 817–824, Sydney, Australia, July.

Kevin Knight and Jonathan Graehl. 1998. Machine transliteration. *Computational Linguistics*, 24(4).

P. Koehn, F. J. Och, and D. Marcu. 2003. Statistical phrase-based translation. In *Proc. HLT-NAACL*.

Grzegorz Kondrak, Xingkai Li, and Mohammad Salameh. 2012. Transliteration experiments on chinese and arabic. In *Proc. Named Entities Workshop at ACL 2012*.

A Kumaran and T. Kellner. 2007. A generic framework for machine transliteration. In *Proc. SIGIR*, pages 721–722.

Chan-Hung Kuo, Shih-Hung Liu, Mike Tian-Jian Jiang, Cheng-Wei Lee, and Wen-Lian Hsu. 2012. Cost-benefit analysis of two-stage conditional random fields based english-to-chinese machine transliteration. In *Proc. Named Entities Workshop at ACL 2012*.

Haizhou Li, Min Zhang, and Jian Su. 2004. A joint source-channel model for machine transliteration. In *Proc. 42nd ACL Annual Meeting*, pages 159–166, Barcelona, Spain.

Haizhou Li, A Kumaran, Vladimir Pervouchine, and Min Zhang. 2009a. Report of NEWS 2009 machine transliteration shared task. In *Proc. Named Entities Workshop at ACL 2009*.

Haizhou Li, A Kumaran, Min Zhang, and Vladimir Pervouchine. 2009b. ACL-IJCNLP 2009 Named Entities Workshop — Shared Task on Transliteration. In *Proc. Named Entities Workshop at ACL 2009*.

Haizhou Li, A Kumaran, Min Zhang, and Vladimir Pervouchine. 2010a. Report of news 2010 transliteration generation shared task. In *Proc. Named Entities Workshop at ACL 2010*.

Haizhou Li, A Kumaran, Min Zhang, and Vladimir Pervouchine. 2010b. Whitepaper of news 2010 shared task on transliteration generation. In *Proc. Named Entities Workshop at ACL 2010*.

T. Mandl and C. Womser-Hacker. 2005. The effect of named entities on effectiveness in cross-language information retrieval evaluation. In *Proc. ACM Symp. Applied Comp.*, pages 1059–1064.

Helen M. Meng, Wai-Kit Lo, Berlin Chen, and Karen Tang. 2001. Generate phonetic cognates to handle name entities in English-Chinese cross-language spoken document retrieval. In *Proc. ASRU*.

MSRI. 2009. Microsoft Research India. http://research.microsoft.com/india.

Jong-Hoon Oh and Key-Sun Choi. 2002. An English-Korean transliteration model using pronunciation and contextual rules. In *Proc. COLING 2002*, Taipei, Taiwan.

Yoh Okuno. 2012. Applying mpaligner to machine transliteration with japanese-specific heuristics. In *Proc. Named Entities Workshop at ACL 2012*.

Tarek Sherif and Grzegorz Kondrak. 2007. Substring-based transliteration. In *Proc. 45th Annual Meeting of the ACL*, pages 944–951, Prague, Czech Republic, June.

Richard Sproat, Tao Tao, and ChengXiang Zhai. 2006. Named entity transliteration with comparable corpora. In *Proc. 21st Int'l Conf Computational Linguistics and 44th Annual Meeting of ACL*, pages 73–80, Sydney, Australia.

Raghavendra Udupa, K. Saravanan, Anton Bakalov, and Abhijit Bhole. 2009. "They are out there, if you know where to look": Mining transliterations of OOV query terms for cross-language information retrieval. In *LNCS: Advances in Information Retrieval*, volume 5478, pages 437–448. Springer Berlin / Heidelberg.

Paola Virga and Sanjeev Khudanpur. 2003. Transliteration of proper names in cross-lingual information retrieval. In *Proc. ACL MLNER*, Sapporo, Japan.

Stephen Wan and Cornelia Maria Verspoor. 1998. Automatic English-Chinese name transliteration for development of multilingual resources. In *Proc. COLING*, pages 1352–1356.

Chun-Kai Wu, Yu-Chun Wang, and Richard Tzong-Han Tsai. 2012. English-korean named entity transliteration using substring alignment and reranking methods. In *Proc. Named Entities Workshop at ACL 2012*.

Dmitry Zelenko and Chinatsu Aone. 2006. Discriminative methods for transliteration. In *Proc. EMNLP*, pages 612–617, Sydney, Australia, July.

Min Zhang, A Kumaran, and Haizhou Li. 2011a. Whitepaper of news 2011 shared task on machine transliteration. In *Proc. Named Entities Workshop at IJCNLP 2011*.

Min Zhang, Haizhou Li, A Kumaran, and Ming Liu. 2011b. Report of news 2011 machine transliteration shared task. In *Proc. Named Entities Workshop at IJCNLP 2011*.

Chunyue Zhang, Tingting Li, and Tiejun Zhao. 2012. Syllable-based machine transliteration with extra phrase features. In *Proc. Named Entities Workshop at ACL 2012*.

Team ID	ACC	F-score	MRR	MAP_{ref}	Organisation
			Primary runs		
3	0.330357	0.66898	0.413062	0.320285	MIT@Lab of HIT
1	0.325397	0.67228	0.418079	0.316296	University of Alberta
2	0.310516	0.66585	0.44664	0.307788	NICT
4	0.310516	0.662467	0.37696	0.299266	IASL, Academia Sinica
5	0.300595	0.655091	0.376025	0.292252	Yahoo Japan Corporation
7	0.031746	0.430698	0.055574	0.030265	CMU
			Non-primary standard runs		
3	0.330357	0.676232	0.407755	0.3191	MIT@Lab of HIT
1	0.325397	0.673053	0.409452	0.316055	University of Alberta
1	0.324405	0.668165	0.424517	0.316248	University of Alberta
3	0.31746	0.666551	0.399476	0.308187	MIT@Lab of HIT
4	0.298611	0.658836	0.362263	0.288725	IASL, Academia Sinica
5	0.298611	0.656974	0.357481	0.289373	Yahoo Japan Corporation
4	0.294643	0.651988	0.357495	0.284274	IASL, Academia Sinica
4	0.290675	0.653565	0.370733	0.282545	IASL, Academia Sinica

Table 4: Runs submitted for English to Chinese task.

Team ID	ACC	F-score	MRR	MAP_{ref}	Organisation
			Primary runs		
2	0.20314	0.736058	0.308801	0.199569	NICT
3	0.176644	0.701791	0.257324	0.172991	MIT@Lab of HIT
7	0.030422	0.489705	0.048211	0.03004	CMU
5	0.012758	0.258962	0.017354	0.012758	Yahoo Japan Corporation
			Non-primary standard runs		
5	0.007851	0.258013	0.012163	0.007851	Yahoo Japan Corporation

Table 5: Runs submitted for Chinese to English back-transliteration task.

Team ID	ACC	F-score	MRR	MAP_{ref}	Organisation
			Primary runs		
2	0.122168	0.746824	0.183318	0.122168	NICT
7	0.000809	0.288585	0.001883	0.000809	CMU

Table 6: Runs submitted for English to Thai task.

Team ID	ACC	F-score	MRR	MAP_{ref}	Organisation
			Primary runs		
2	0.139968	0.765534	0.21551	0.139968	NICT
7	0	0.417451	0.000566	0	CMU

Table 7: Runs submitted for Thai to English back-transliteration task.

Team ID	ACC	F-score	MRR	MAP_{ref}	Organisation
			Primary runs		
2	0.668	0.923347	0.73795	0.661278	NICT
7	0.048	0.645666	0.087842	0.048528	CMU

Table 8: Runs submitted for English to Hindi task.

Team ID	ACC	F-score	MRR	MAP_{ref}	Organisation
			Primary runs		
2	0.592	0.908444	0.67881	0.5915	NICT
7	0.052	0.638029	0.083728	0.052	CMU

Table 9: Runs submitted for English to Tamil task.

Team ID	ACC	F-score	MRR	MAP_{ref}	Organisation
			Primary runs		
2	0.546	0.900557	0.640534	0.545361	NICT
7	0.116	0.737857	0.180234	0.11625	CMU

Table 10: Runs submitted for English to Kannada task.

Team ID	ACC	F-score	MRR	MAP_{ref}	Organisation
			Primary runs		
2	0.400774	0.810109	0.522758	0.397386	NICT
5	0.362052	0.802701	0.468973	0.35939	Yahoo Japan Corporation
7	0	0.147441	0.00038	0	CMU

Table 11: Runs submitted for English to Japanese Katakana task.

Team ID	ACC	F-score	MRR	MAP_{ref}	Organisation
			Primary runs		
6	0.398095	0.731212	0.398095	0.396905	Yuan Ze University
2	0.38381	0.721247	0.464553	0.383095	NICT
5	0.334286	0.687794	0.411264	0.334048	Yahoo Japan Corporation
7	0	0	0.00019	0	CMU
			Non-standard runs		
6	0.458095	0.756755	0.484048	0.458095	Yuan Ze University

Table 12: Runs submitted for English to Korean task.

Team ID	ACC	F-score	MRR	MAP_{ref}	Organisation
			Primary runs		
2	0.513242	0.693184	0.598304	0.418708	NICT
5	0.512329	0.693029	0.581803	0.400505	Yahoo Japan Corporation
7	0	0	0	0	CMU
			Non-primary standard runs		
5	0.511416	0.691131	0.580485	0.402127	Yahoo Japan Corporation

Table 13: Runs submitted for English to Japanese Kanji back-transliteration task.

Team ID	ACC	F-score	MRR	MAP_{ref}	Organisation
			Primary runs		
2	0.588235	0.929787	0.709003	0.506991	NICT
7	0.58391	0.925292	0.694338	0.367162	CMU
1	0.583045	0.932959	0.670457	0.42041	University of Alberta
			Non-primary standard runs		
7	0.57699	0.93025	0.678898	0.330353	CMU
7	0.573529	0.925306	0.675125	0.328782	CMU

Table 14: Runs submitted for Arabic to English task.

Team ID	ACC	F-score	MRR	MAP_{ref}	Organisation
			Primary runs		
2	0.46	0.891476	0.582944	0.458417	NICT
5	0.404	0.882395	0.514541	0.402917	Yahoo Japan Corporation
7	0.178	0.783893	0.248674	0.177139	CMU
			Non-primary standard runs		
5	0.398	0.880286	0.510148	0.396528	Yahoo Japan Corporation

Table 15: Runs submitted for English to Bengali (Bangla) task.

Team ID	ACC	F-score	MRR	MAP_{ref}	Organisation
			Primary runs		
5	0.658349	0.940642	0.761223	0.639873	Yahoo Japan Corporation
2	0.65547	0.941044	0.773843	0.642663	NICT
7	0.18618	0.803002	0.311881	0.184961	CMU
			Non-primary standard runs		
5	0.054702	0.627335	0.082754	0.054367	Yahoo Japan Corporation

Table 16: Runs submitted for English to Persian task.

Team ID	ACC	F-score	MRR	MAP_{ref}	Organisation
			Primary runs		
5	0.190909	0.808491	0.253575	0.19	Yahoo Japan Corporation
2	0.153636	0.787254	0.228649	0.152727	NICT
7	0.097273	0.759444	0.130955	0.096818	CMU
			Non-primary standard runs		
5	0.165455	0.803019	0.241948	0.164545	Yahoo Japan Corporation

Table 17: Runs submitted for English to Hebrew task.

Accurate Unsupervised Joint Named-Entity Extraction from Unaligned Parallel Text

Robert Munro
Department of Linguistics
Stanford University
Stanford, CA 94305
rmunro@stanford.edu

Christopher D. Manning
Department of Computer Science
Stanford University
Stanford, CA 94305
manning@stanford.edu

Abstract

We present a new approach to named-entity recognition that jointly learns to identify named-entities in parallel text. The system generates seed candidates through local, cross-language edit likelihood and then bootstraps to make broad predictions across both languages, optimizing combined contextual, word-shape and alignment models. It is completely unsupervised, with no manually labeled items, no external resources, only using parallel text that does not need to be easily alignable. The results are strong, with $F > 0.85$ for purely unsupervised named-entity recognition across languages, compared to just $F = 0.35$ on the same data for supervised cross-domain named-entity recognition within a language. A combination of unsupervised and supervised methods increases the accuracy to $F = 0.88$. We conclude that we have found a viable new strategy for unsupervised named-entity recognition across low-resource languages and for domain-adaptation within high-resource languages.

1 Introduction

At first pass, our approach sounds like it shouldn't work, as *'unsupervised'* tasks significantly underperform their supervised equivalents and for most cross-linguistic tasks *'unaligned'* will mean *'unusable'*. However, even among very loosely aligned multilingual text it is easy to see why named-entities are different: they are the least likely words/phrases to change form in translation. We can see this in the following example which shows the named-entities in both a Krèyol message and its English translation:

> <u>Lopital Sacre-Coeur</u> ki nan vil <u>Milot</u>, 14 km nan sid vil <u>Okap</u>, pre pou li resevwa moun malad e lap mande pou moun ki malad yo ale la.
>
> <u>Sacre-Coeur Hospital</u> which located in this village <u>Milot</u> 14 km south of <u>Oakp</u> is ready to receive those who are injured. Therefore, we are asking those who are sick to report to that hospital.

The example is taken from the parallel corpus of English and Haitian Krèyol text messages used in the *2010 Shared Task for the Workshop on Machine Translation* (Callison-Burch et al., 2011), which is the corpus used for evaluation in this paper.

The similarities in the named-entities across the translation are clear, as should be the intuition for how we can leverage these for named-entity extraction. Phrases with the least edit distance between the two languages, such as *'Lopital Sacre-Coeur'*, *'Milot'*, and *'Okap'*, can be treated as high-probability named-entity candidates, and then a model can be bootstrapped that exploits predictive features, such as word shape (e.g.: more frequent capitalization) and contextual cues such as the preceding *'vil'* in two cases above.

However, the problem of identifying entities in this way is non-trivial due to a number of complicating factors. The inexact translation repeats the non-entity *'hospital'* which limits machine-translation-style alignments and has an equal edit-distance with the entity *'Loptial'*. The entity *'Hospital'* and *'Lopital'* are not an exact match and are not perfectly aligned, changing position within the phrase. The capitalization of entities is not always so consistent (here and in short-message communications more generally). A typographic error in the translation writes *'Okap'* as *'Oakp'*. *'Okap'* is itself slang for *'Cap-Haïtien'* and other messages translated this location across the different spellings (*'Cap-Haitien'*, *'Cap Haitien'*, *'Kap'*, *'Kapayisyen'*, etc.), which increases the edit distance. There are few resources for Haitian Krèyol such as gazatteers of place names (except at the Department/major Town/City level – at the time these messages were sent, *Google Maps* and *Open Street Map* listed only a handful of locations in Haiti, and such resources tend not to include slang terms). Finally, what was one sentence in the original message is split into two in the translation.

As Kay points out, most parallel texts *shouldn't* be alignable, as different contexts mean different translation strategies, most of which will not result in usable input for machine translation (Kay, 2006). This is true of the corpus used here – the translations were made for quick understanding by aid workers, explaining much of the above: it was clearer to break the translation into two sentences; it reduced ambiguity to repeat 'hospital' rather than leave it underspecified; the typo simply didn't matter. We confirmed the 'unalignability' of this corpus using the *GIZA++* aligner in the *Moses* toolkit (Koehn et al., 2007); by noting *Microsoft Research*'s work on the same data where they needed to carefully retranslate the messages for training (Lewis, 2010); and from correspondence with participants in the *2011 Workshop on Machine Translation* who reported the need for substantial preprocessing and mixed results.

We do not rule out the alignability of the corpus altogether – the system presented here could even be used to create better alignment models – noting only that it is rare that translations can be used straight-of-the-box, while in our case we *can* still make use of this data. Even with perfect alignment, the accuracy for named-entity extraction in Haitian Krèyol could only be as accurate as that for English, which in this case was $F = 0.336$ with a supervised model, so alignment is therefore only part of the problem.

For the same reasons, we are deliberately omitting another important aspect of cross-linguistic named-entity recognition: *transliteration*. Latin Script may be wide-spread, especially for low resource languages where it is the most common script for transcribing previously non-written languages, but some of the most widely spoken languages include those that use Arabic, Bengali, Cyrillic, Devanagari (Hindi) and Hanzi (Chinese) scripts, and the methods proposed here would be even richer if they could also identify named entities across scripts. A first pass on cross-script data looks like it *is* possible to apply our methods across scripts, especially because the seeds only need to be drawn from the most confident matches and across scripts there seem to be some named entities that are more easier to transliterate than others (which is not surprising, of course – most cross-linguistic tasks are heterogeneous in this way). However, with a few notable exceptions like Tao et al. (2006), transliteration is typically a supervised task. As with machine translation it is likely that the methods used here could aid transliteration, providing predictions that can be used within a final, supervised transliteration model (much like the semi-supervised model proposed later on).[1]

1.1 The limitations of edit-distance and supervised approaches

Despite the intuition that named-entities are less likely to change form across translations, it is clearly only a weak trend. Even if we assume oracle knowledge of entities in English (that is, imagining that we have perfect named-entity-recognition for English), by mapping the lowest edit-distance phrase in the parallel Krèyol message to each entity we can only identify an entity with about 61%, accuracy. *Without* oracle knowledge – training on an existing English NER corpora, tagging the English translations, and mapping via edit distance – identifies an entity with only around 15% accuracy. This is not particularly useful and we could probably achieve the same results with naive techniques like cross-linguistic gazetteers.

Edit distance and cross-linguistic supervised named-entity recognition are *not*, therefore, particularly useful as standalone strategies. However, we are able to use aspects of both in an unsupervised approach.

[1]On a more practical level, we also note that this year's shared task for the Named Entity Workshop is on transliteration. With the leading researchers in the field currently tackling the transliteration problem, it is likely that any methods we presented here would soon be outdated.

In this paper we focus on named-entity identification, only briefly touching on named-entity classification (distinguishing between types of entities), primarily because the named-entity identification component of our system is more novel and therefore deserves greater attention.

We use 3,000 messages in Haitian Krèyol and their English translations, with named-entities tagged in an evaluation set of 1,000 of the messages. To keep the task as unsupervised a possible, the system was designed and parameters were set without observing the actual tags.

1.2 Strategy and potential applications

Our approach is two-step for pairs of low resource languages, and three-step for pairs of languages where one has named-entity resources:

1. *Generate seeds by calculating the edit likelihood deviation.* For all cross-language pairs of messages, extract the cross-language word/phrase pairs with the highest edit likelihood, normalized for length. Calculate the intramessage deviation of this edit likelihood from the mean pair-wise likelihood from all candidate pairs within the message. Across all messages, generate seeds by selecting the word/phrase pairs with the highest and lowest intramessage edit likelihood deviation.
2. *Learn context, word-shape and alignment models.* Using the seeds from Step 1, learn models over the context, word-shape and alignment properties (but not edit distance). Apply the models to all candidate pairs. Because we have the candidate alignments between the languages, we can also jointly learn to identify named-entities by leveraging the context and word-shape features in the parallel text, in combination with the alignment predictions.
3. *Learn weighted models over the context, word-shape, alignment and supervised predictions (with high-resource languages only).* Using the seeds from Step 1 and predictions from Step 2, learn models over the broader features and supervised predictions from a model in the high-resource language, applying the models to all candidate pairs.

The results are very strong, with $F > 0.85$ for purely unsupervised named-entity recognition across languages. This is compared to just $F = 0.35$ for supervised approaches across domains within a language (MUC/CoNLL-trained English applied to the English translations of the messages).

The combined unsupervised/supervised methods increase the accuracy to $F = 0.88$. Inter-annotator agreement is around 0.95, so this may be close to the best possible result.

This leads us to conclude that cross-linguistic unsupervised named-entity recognition, even when not alignable via machine-translation methods, is a powerful, scalable technique for named-entity recognition in low resource languages.

The potential applications of are broad. There are some 5,000 languages in the connected world, most of which will have no resources *other* than loose translations, so there is great application potential. For high-resource languages, the results here indicate that the technique can be used to increase accuracy in cross-domain named-entity recognition, a consistent problem across even closely-related domains. For the specific corpus used there is also direct practical value – the messages include high volumes of time-critical requests for aid, citing locations that did not appear on any map in a language with few resources.

2 STEP 1: Establish Edit Likelihood Deviation

As we state in the introduction, we cannot simply tag in English and then find the least-edit distance word/phrase in the parallel Krèyol.

We evaluated several different edit distance functions, including the well-known Levenshtein and slightly more complex Jaro-Winkler measures. We also extended the Levenshtein measure by reducing the edit penalty for pairs of letters of phonetic relatedness, such as '*c*' and '*k*', following the subword modeling work of Munro and Manning on this corpus and previous subword modeling for short messages (Munro, 2011; Munro and Manning, 2010).[2]

[2]We also attempted a more sophisticated approach to learning weights for edits by extracting edit probabilities from the final model. This also made little improvement, but it could have simply been the result data-sparseness over only 3000 pairs of entities, so no strong conclusions can be drawn.

The more sophisticated edit distance functions gave more accurate predictions (which is unsurprising), but the advantages were lost in the following step when calculating the deviation from the norm, with all approaches producing more or less the same seeds. Rather than the String Similarity Estimate being the key factor, we conclude that our novel treatment of edit distance (calculating the local deviation) is the critical factor in generating seeds for the model.

All else being equal, then, we report results from the *simplest* approach to edit distance, normalizing Levenshtein's measure, $LEV()$ by length to a 0-1 scale. Candidate words/phrases were limited to a maximum of four words, delimited by space or punctuation, simply to cap the cost of the $LEV()$. Given a string S in message M, M_S and and its candidate pair $M'_{S'}$, and a length function $LEN()$, this gives us $SSE(M_S, M'_{S'}) =$

$$1 - \frac{(2(LEV(M_S, M'_{S'})) + 1}{LEN(M_S) + LEN(M'_{S'}) + 1}$$

The $+1$ smoothing is to avoid too much variation at smaller lengths, which is fairly common practice in subword models looking at morphological variation (Tchoukalov et al., 2010).

The String Similarity Estimate is a global measure that is not sensitive to the contexts of the given pairs. Suppose a sentence *wasn't* a translation, but simply a repetition, or that much of the translation was a direct (non-translated) quote of the original. Both occur in the data we used.

We propose, then, that the best candidate seeds for named-entities are those that display the highest likelihood relative to the other candidate pairs within the same pairs of messages. In other words, when there are two phrases with very little edit distance, but when there is very high cross-language edit distance between the contexts of the phrases. We define this as *Edit Likelihood Deviation*, $ELD()$.

There are many ways to calculating deviation. Again, to keep it as simple as possible we report results using the most well-known deviation metric, z-scores. Given average and standard deviation functions $AV()$ and $SD()$, gives $ELD(M_S, M'_{S'}) =$

$$\frac{(SSE(M_S, M'_{S'})) - AV(SSE(M_{0-n}, M'_{0-m}))}{SD(SSE(M_{0-n}, M'_{0-m}))}$$

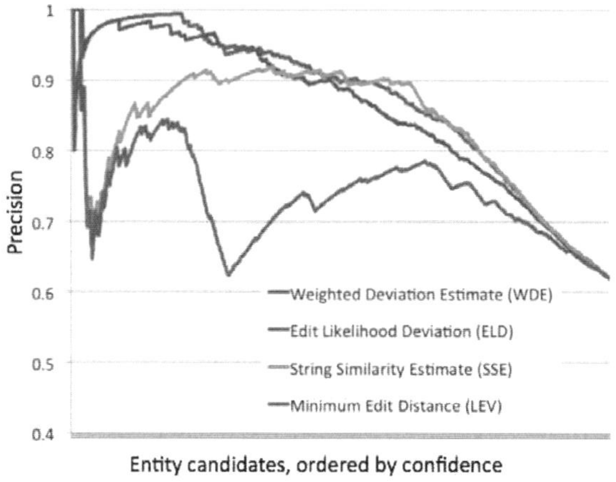

Figure 1: A comparison of the different approaches to generating seeds from edit distance. The comparison shows that local deviation, the novel method introduced in this paper, is the most successful. With about 10% of the most confident entity candidates by Edit Likelihood Deviation or Weighted Deviation Estimate, there is greater than 95% precision, giving a clean enough division of the data to seed a model.

At this point, we have the global string similarity of each candidate entity pair across languages, $SSE()$, and the local string similarity deviation of each candidate pair, $ELD()$.

A combination was also explored that combined the two, creating an equally weighted product of SSE and $ELD()$, *Weighted Deviation Estimate*, $WDE()$ (equation omitted for space). As Figure 1 shows, there is only a slight improvement from the combination of the two, showing that *Edit Likelihood Deviation*, the novel approach here, contributes the most to identifying candidate seeds.

We can calculate the first accuracies here by assuming that the best candidate in each message pair was an entity. All results also summarized at the end of the paper:

	Precision	**Recall**	**F-value**
Krèyol:	0.619	0.619	0.619
English:	0.633	0.633	0.633

The results are reasonably strong for methods that made few assumptions about the data and were not optimized, with errors in a little under half the predictions.

While the different equations are monotonically distributed *within* each pair of messages, the estimates *between* messages now take into account both local and global edit likelihoods, allowing us to rank the candidates by WDE and sample the most likely and least likely. Here, we simply took the top and bottom 5%.[3]

3 STEP 2: Learn joint alignment and word-shape models using the likelihood estimates as seeds.

Taking the seeds from Step 1, we can then treat them as training items in a linear model.

We used the Stanford Maximum Entropy Classifier. Model-choice is only important in that a discriminative learner is required. The 5% 'non-entity' pairs were still the highest String Similarity for their particular message/translation, but simply did not deviate greatly from the average within that message/translation. Therefore, we are explicitly targeting the border between entities and non-entities in the high String Similarity part of the vector space. This sampling strategy would not work for a generative learner.

For the same reason, though, we do *not* include raw edit distance or the String Similarity Estimate among the features. If we did, then the model will simply relearn and overfit this bias and give all the weight to edit distance.

We build the model on features that include context (the entity itself and surrounding words), word-shape features (capitalization, punctuation, segmentation, and numerical patterns), and alignment (absolute and relative character offsets between the candidates in the messages and translation). For word-shape features, we used a simple representation that converted all sequences of capitalized letters, lower-case letters, and non-letter characters into 'C', 'c' and 'n', respectively. Therefore, 'Port-au-Prince', 'Port au Prince' and 'Port.a.Prons' would all get the same word-shape feature, 'CcncnCc'. We allowed the model to also find character-ngrams over these shapes to capture features which would represent characteristics like 'is-capitalized', 'contains-internal-capital', and 'is-multiword-phrase'.

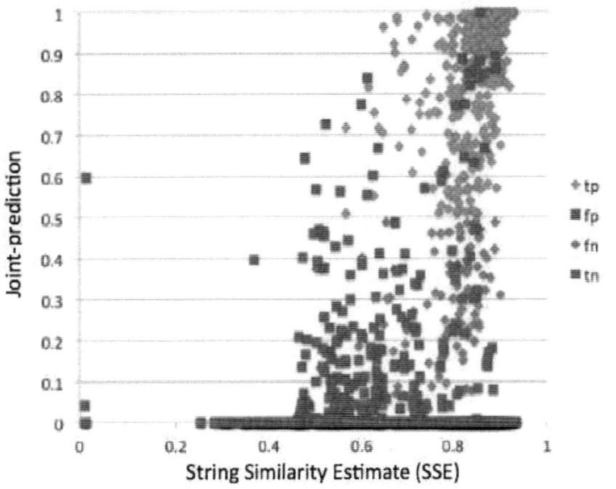

Figure 2: Comparing the predictions for the String Similarity for the same candidates, to the jointly-learned model. (Coding scheme: tp = true-positive, etc.) The distribution shows that while String Similarity correlates with named-entities, it is not a clean division. Note especially the mass of true-negatives in the bottom-right corner of the graph. These would be a relatively high volume of false-positives for String Similarity alone, but the model that bootstraps knowledge of context, word-shape and alignment has little trouble distinguishing them and correctly assigning them zero-probably of being an entity.

As a relatively small set of features, we also model the intersection of each of them. This allows the model to learn, for example, that words that are perfectly aligned, but are both all lower-case, are weighted 0.06 more likely as a non-entity. Despite the simplicity and low number of features, this is a fairly powerful concept to model.

As with all unsupervised methods that bootstrap predictions through seeded data, the success relies on a representative feature space to avoid learning only one part of the problem. The results are strong:

	Precision	Recall	F-value
Krèyol:	0.907	0.687	0.781
English:	0.932	0.766	0.840

There is a reasonably high precision-recall ratio which is typical of unsupervised learning that learns a model on seeded data, but the results are still

[3] There are clearly many more parameters and variants of equations that could be explored. As an unsupervised approach, it is by conscious choice that only the most well-known equations are used and tunable parameters are set at sensible defaults (like the equal weights here). This is to keep the experiments as cleanly 'unsupervised' as possible, and to demonstrate that the accurate results here are not simply a quirk of a particular equation, but a broadly applicable approach to generating seeds by local deviation estimates.

strong for both Krèyol and English, indicating that the seeding method in Step 1 did, in fact, produce candidates that occurred in broad range of contexts, overcoming one of the limits of gazetteer-based approaches.

Perhaps the most obvious extension is to jointly learn the models on both languages, using the candidate alignment models in combination with the contexts in both the original text and the translation:

	Precision	Recall	F-value
Krèyol:	0.904	0.794	0.846
English:	0.915	0.813	0.861

This improves the results for both, especially the Krèyol which can now take advantage of the more consistent capitalization and spelling in the English translations.

For many supervised learners, 0.846 would be a strong result. Here, we are able to get this in Hatian Krèyol using only unsupervised methods and a few thousand loosely translated sentences.

4 STEP 3: Learning weighted models over the context, word-shape, alignment and supervised predictions (with high-resource languages)

The natural extension to the supervised comparison is to combine the methods. We included the Stanford NER predictions in the features for the final model, allowing the bootstrapped model to arrive at the optimal weights to apply to the supervised predictions in the given context.

From the perspective of supervised NER, this can be thought of as leveraging unsupervised alignment models for domain-adaptation. The Stanford NER predictions were added as features in the final model, directly for the English phrases and across the candidate alignments for the Krèyol phrases.

Taken alone, the unsupervised strategies clearly improve the results, but for someone coming from a supervised learning background in NER (which will be most NER researchers) this should provide an intuition as to exactly how good. We cannot compare the Krèyol as there is no supervised NER corpus for Krèyol, and our labeled evaluation data is too small to train on. However, we can compare the English results to near state-of-the-art NER taggers.

We compared our system to the predictions made by the Stanford NER parser trained on MUC and CoNLL data (Sang, 2002; Sang and De Meulder, 2003):

	Precision	Recall	F-value
English:	0.915	0.206	0.336

The low cross-domain result is expected, but 0.336 for supervised cross-domain predictions within a language is *much* less than 0.861 for unsupervised cross-language predictions. This clearly shows that the methods and evaluation used here really do demonstrate a new strategy for NER. It also shows that domain-specificity might be even be more important than language-specificity when we can bootstrap our knowledge of context.[4]

Combining the two approaches, we get the most accurate results:

	Precision	Recall	F-value
Krèyol:	0.838	0.902	0.869
English:	0.846	0.916	0.880

Even though English is a high-resource language, this is still a very good result for cross-domain adaptation, with $F > 0.5$ improvement over the supervised model alone. It is clear that this strategy could be used for domain adaptation more broadly wherever loose translations exists.

While not as big a gain in accuracy as the previous steps, the $F > 0.02$ gain is still significant. Although untested here, it is easy to imagine that with a small amount of labeled data or improved gazetteers the supervised approach should further. About 10% of the error can be attributed to capitalization, too, which is a slight bias against the MUC/CoNLL trained data where the capitalization of named entities was consistent. A realistic deployment approach would be to create an initial model using the unsupervised methods described in this paper and then to further bootstrap the accuracy through supervised labeling. This particular approach to semi-supervised learning is outside the scope of this paper.

[4]For the edge cases and entity boundary errors, we always gave the benefit of the doubt to the Stanford NER tagger.

4.1 Distinguishing Types of Entity

NER often distinguishes types of Entities (eg: People, Locations, Organizations); a frequent subtask sometimes called *named-entity discrimination* or *named-entity classification*. We discuss this briefly.

By seeding the data with the Stanford NER predictions for 'Person', 'Location', and 'Organization' and learning a three-way distinction within the entities, we saw that it wasn't a difficult problem for this particular corpus. The main potential complication was between organizations and locations (especially for radio stations) but there were relatively few organizations in the data so the micro-fvalue would change very little. No doubt, in other texts the location/organization division would compose a bigger part of the problem. These observations about distinguishing NERs are consistent with the known problems in NER more broadly. The Stanford NER only made predictions for 114 of the entities that were confidently mapped to their Krèyol counterparts in Step 1:

	Precision	**Recall**	**F-value**
English:	0.512	0.782	0.619

To exploit *any* signal here, let alone a respectable $F = 0.619$ is a good result, but clearly more improvements are possible.

5 Analysis

The results presented in the paper are summarized in Table 1. Taken together, they make it clear that this is a very promising new method for named-entity recognition in low resources languages, and for domain-adaptation in high-resource languages.

Analysis of the consistent errors shows several clear patterns. Products like *'aquatab'* were a common false positive, although a product could be a named-entity in certain coding schemas. Dates, figures and currency (*'250gd'*) were also frequent false positives, but would be reasonably easy to filter as they follow predictable patterns.

Some cognates and borrowings also made it through as false-positives: *'antibiotics'/'antibiotik'*, *'drinking water'/'drinking water'*, *'medicine'/'medicament'*, *'vitamin c'/'vitamine c'*, *'cyber'/'cyber'*, *'radio'/'radyo'*, although *'cyber cafe'* almost always referred to a specific location and *'radio'* was often part of an organization name, *'radio enspirasyon'*.

The false-negatives were almost all very low-frequency words or high-frequency words that were more commonly used as non-entities. This is consistent with named-entity recognition more broadly.

6 Background and Related Work

We were surprised that no one had previously reported looked at leveraging cross-linguistic named-entity recognition in this way. Perhaps previous researchers had found (like us) that edit distance alone was not particularly useful in cross-linguistic named-entity recognition, and therefore not pursued it. While the approach is novel, the general observation that named-entities change form less than other words cross-linguistically is one of the oldest in language studies. Shakespeare's 'River Avon' simply means 'River River', as 'Avon' is, literally, 'River' in the pre-English Celtic language of the region.

For parallel short-message corpora, named-entity recognition is completely unresearched, but there is growing work in classification (Munro and Manning, 2010; Munro, 2011) and translation (Lewis, 2010), the latter two using the same corpus as here.

Past *'Multilingual Named-Entity Recognition'* systems meant training the same supervised system on different languages, which was the focus of the past CoNLL tasks. While the goal of these systems was the same as ours – broad cross-linguistic coverage for named-entity recognition – this is *not* the same 'cross-linguistic' as the one employed here.

More closely related to our work, Steinberger and Pouliquen have found cross-linguistic named-entity recognition to be possible by aligning texts at the granularity of news stories (Steinberger and Pouliquen, 2007), but using a supervised approach for the first pass and focusing on transliteration. In other related work, the 2007 NIST *REFLEX* evaluation (Song and Strassel, 2008), tasked participants with using alignment models to map named-entities between English, Arabic, and Chinese data. They found that relying on alignment models alone was very poor, even among these high-resource languages, although it was a relatively small corpus (about 1,000 aligned entities). The focus was more on transliteration – an important aspect of translation that we simply aren't addressing here.

Most earlier work used a tagger in one language in combination with machine translation-style alignments models. Among these, Huang et al. is the most closely related to our work as they are translating rare named-entities, and are therefore in a similar low-resource context (Huang et al., 2004). As with the *NIST* project, most work building on Huang et al. has been in transliteration.

Although not cross-linguistic, Piskorski et al.'s work on NER for inflectional languages (2009) also relied on the similarities in edit distance between the *intra*-language variation of names.

In gazetteer-related work, Wang et al. and others since, have looked at edit distance within a language, modeling the distance between observed words and lists of entities (Wang et al., 2009). Similarly, there is a cluster of slightly older work on unsupervised entity detection, also within one language (Pedersen et al., 2006; Nadeau et al., 2006), but all relying on web-scale quantities of unlabeled data.

While the implementation is not related, it is also worth highlighting Lin et al.'s very recent work on unsupervised language-independent name translation the mines data from Wikipedia 'infoboxes', (Lin et al., 2011) however the infoboxes give a fairly and highly structured resource, that might be considered more supervised than not.

In alignment work, the foundational work is Yarowsky et al.'s induction of projections across aligned corpora (Yarowsky et al., 2001), most successfully adapted to cross-linguistic syntactic parsing (Hwa et al., 2005). The machine translation systems used named-entity recognition are too many to list here, but as we say, the system we present could aid translation considerably, especially in the context of low resources languages and humanitarian contexts, a recent focus in the field (Callison-Burch et al., 2011; Lewis et al., 2011).

7 Conclusions

We have presented a promising a new strategy for named-entity recognition from unaligned parallel corpora, finding that unsupervised named-entity recognition across languages can be bootstrapped from calculating the local edit distance deviation between candidate entities. Purely unsupervised approaches are able to identify named entities with $F = 0.846$ accuracy for Krèyol and $F = 0.861$ for English, leveraging the candidate alignments for improved accuracy in both cases. Combined with supervised learning, the accuracy rises to $F = 0.869$ and $F = 0.880$ respectively, which is approaching the level of accuracy achieved by in-domain supervised systems. It is rare for unsupervised systems to be competitive with supervised approaches as accuracy is usually lost for coverage, but here it looks like the method can be effective for both.

Unsupervised	**Precision**	**Recall**	**F-value**
Edit likelihood deviation			
Krèyol:	0.619	0.619	0.619
English:	0.633	0.633	0.633
Language-specific models			
Krèyol:	0.907	0.687	0.781
English:	0.932	0.766	0.840
Jointly-learned models			
Krèyol:	0.904	0.794	**0.846**
English:	0.915	0.813	**0.861**
Supervised			
English:	0.915	0.206	0.336
Semi-supervised			
Identification			
Krèyol:	0.838	0.902	**0.869**
English:	0.846	0.916	**0.880**
Classification (micro-F)			
English:	0.512	0.782	0.619

Table 1: A summary of the results presented in this paper showing promising new methods for unsupervised and semi-supervised named-entity recognition.

There is the potential to apply this system to a large number of natural language processing problems, and to extend the system in a number of directions. Each of the three steps has parameters that could be optimized, especially in combination with supervised approaches. The linguistic nature of the language pairs might also influence the effectiveness. The results here are therefore the first presentation of a new strategy – one that will hopefully lead to more research in extracting rich information from a diverse range of low-resource languages.

References

C.. Callison-Burch, P. Koehn, C. Monz, and Zaidan. O. 2011. Findings of the 2011 workshop on statistical machine translation. In *Proceedings of the Sixth Workshop on Statistical Machine Translation*.

F. Huang, S. Vogel, and A. Waibel. 2004. Improving named entity translation combining phonetic and semantic similarities. In *Proc. of HLT-NAACL*, pages 281–288.

R. Hwa, P. Resnik, A. Weinberg, C. Cabezas, and O. Kolak. 2005. Bootstrapping parsers via syntactic projection across parallel texts. *Natural language engineering*, 11(3):311–325.

M. Kay. 2006. Translation, Meaning and Reference. *Intelligent Linguistic Architectures: Variations on Themes by Ronald M. Kaplan*, page 3.

P. Koehn, H. Hoang, A. Birch, C. Callison-Burch, M. Federico, N. Bertoldi, B. Cowan, W. Shen, C. Moran, R. Zens, et al. 2007. Moses: Open source toolkit for statistical machine translation. In *Proceedings of the 45th Annual Meeting of the ACL on Interactive Poster and Demonstration Sessions*, pages 177–180. Association for Computational Linguistics.

W. Lewis, R. Munro, and S. Vogel. 2011. Crisis mt: Developing a cookbook for mt in crisis situations. In *Proceedings of the Sixth Workshop on Statistical Machine Translation*.

W. Lewis. 2010. Haitian Creole: How to Build and Ship an MT Engine from Scratch in 4 days, 17 hours, & 30 minutes. In *14th Annual Conference of the European Association for Machine Translation*.

W.P. Lin, M. Snover, and H. Ji. 2011. Unsupervised Language-Independent Name Translation Mining from Wikipedia Infoboxes. *Proceedings of the EMNLP Workshop on Unsupervised Learning in NLP*, page 43.

R. Munro and C.D. Manning. 2010. Subword variation in text message classification. In *Proceedings of the Annual Conference of the North American Chapter of the Association for Computational Linguistics (NAACL 2010)*.

R. Munro. 2011. Subword and spatiotemporal models for identifying actionable information in haitian kreyol. In *Fifteenth Conference on Computational Natural Language Learning (CoNLL 2011)*.

D. Nadeau, P. Turney, and S. Matwin. 2006. Unsupervised named-entity recognition: Generating gazetteers and resolving ambiguity. *Advances in Artificial Intelligence*, pages 266–277.

T. Pedersen, A. Kulkarni, R. Angheluta, Z. Kozareva, and T. Solorio. 2006. An unsupervised language independent method of name discrimination using second order co-occurrence features. *Computational Linguistics and Intelligent Text Processing*, pages 208–222.

J. Piskorski, K. Wieloch, and M. Sydow. 2009. On knowledge-poor methods for person name matching and lemmatization for highly inflectional languages. *Information retrieval*, 12(3):275–299.

E.F Tjong Kim Sang and F. De Meulder. 2003. Introduction to the CoNLL-2003 shared task: Language-independent named entity recognition. In *Proceedings of the seventh conference on Natural language learning at HLT-NAACL 2003-Volume 4*, pages 142–147. Association for Computational Linguistics.

E.F. Tjong Kim Sang. 2002. Introduction to the CoNLL-2002 shared task: language-independent named entity recognition, proceedings of the 6th conference on natural language learning. *August*, 31:1–4.

Z. Song and S. Strassel. 2008. Entity translation and alignment in the ACE-07 ET task. *Proceedings of LREC-2008*.

R. Steinberger and B. Pouliquen. 2007. Cross-lingual named entity recognition. *Lingvisticæ Investigationes*, 30(1):135–162.

T. Tao, S.Y. Yoon, A. Fister, R. Sproat, and C.X. Zhai. 2006. Unsupervised named entity transliteration using temporal and phonetic correlation. In *Proceedings of the 2006 Conference on Empirical Methods in Natural Language Processing*, pages 250–257. Association for Computational Linguistics.

T. Tchoukalov, C. Monson, and B. Roark. 2010. Morphological analysis by multiple sequence alignment. *Multilingual Information Access Evaluation I. Text Retrieval Experiments*, pages 666–673.

W. Wang, C. Xiao, X. Lin, and C. Zhang. 2009. Efficient approximate entity extraction with edit distance constraints. In *Proceedings of the 35th SIGMOD international conference on Management of data*, pages 759–770. ACM.

D. Yarowsky, G. Ngai, and R. Wicentowski. 2001. Inducing multilingual text analysis tools via robust projection across aligned corpora. In *Proceedings of the first international conference on Human language technology research*, pages 1–8. Association for Computational Linguistics.

Latent Semantic Transliteration using Dirichlet Mixture

Masato Hagiwara **Satoshi Sekine**
Rakuten Institute of Technology, New York
215 Park Avenue South, New York, NY
{masato.hagiwara, satoshi.b.sekine}@mail.rakuten.com

Abstract

Transliteration has been usually recognized by spelling-based supervised models. However, a single model cannot deal with mixture of words with different origins, such as "get" in "piaget" and "target". Li et al. (2007) propose a class transliteration method, which explicitly models the source language origins and switches them to address this issue. In contrast to their model which requires an explicitly tagged training corpus with language origins, Hagiwara and Sekine (2011) have proposed the *latent class transliteration* model, which models language origins as latent classes and train the transliteration table via the EM algorithm. However, this model, which can be formulated as unigram mixture, is prone to overfitting since it is based on maximum likelihood estimation. We propose a novel *latent semantic transliteration* model based on Dirichlet mixture, where a Dirichlet mixture prior is introduced to mitigate the overfitting problem. We have shown that the proposed method considerably outperform the conventional transliteration models.

1 Introduction

Transliteration (e.g., バラクオバマ *baraku obama* "Barak Obama") is phonetic translation between languages with different writing systems, which is a major way of importing foreign words into different languages. Supervised, spelling-based grapheme-to-grapheme models such as (Brill and Moore, 2000; Li et al., 2004), which directly align characters in the training corpus without depending on phonetic information, and statistically computing their correspondence, have been a popular method to detect and/or generate transliterations, in contrast to phonetic-based methods such as (Knight and Jonathan, 1998). However, single, monolithic models fail to deal with sets of foreign words with multiple language origins mixed together. For example, the "get" part of "piaget / ピアジェ *piaje*" and "target / ターゲット *tāgetto*" differ in pronunciation and spelling correspondence depending on their source languages, which are French and English in this case.

To address this issue, Li et al. (2007) have proposed *class transliteration model*, which explicitly models and classifies classes of languages (such as Chinese Hanzi, Japanese Katakana, and so on) and genders, and switches corresponding transliteration models based on the input. This model requires training sets of transliterated word pairs tagged with language origin, which is difficult to obtain. Hagiwara and Sekine proposed the *latent class transliteration (LCT)* model (Hagiwara and Sekine, 2011), which models source language origins as directly unobservable latent classes and applies appropriate transliteration models to given transliteration pairs. The model parameters are learned from corpora without language origins in an unsupervised manner. This enables us to correctly assign latent classes for English and French to "piaget / ピアジェ*piaje*" and "target / ターゲッ

ト *tāgetto*" and to identify their transliteration correspondence correctly. However, this model is based on maximum likelihood estimation on multinomials and thus sensitive to noise in the training data such as transliteration pairs with irregular pronunciation, and tends to overfit the data.

Considering the atomic re-writing unit (transliteration unit, or TU, e.g., "get / ゲット *getto*") as a word, and a transliteration pair as a document consisting of a word sequence, class-based transliteration can be modeled by the perfect analogy to document topic models proposed in tha past. In fact, the LCT model, where the transliteration probability is defined by a mixture of multinomials, can be regarded as a variant of a topic model, namely Unigram Mixuture (UM) (Nigam et al., 2000). There has been an extension of unigram mixture proposed (Sjölander et al., 1996; Yamamoto and Sadamitsu, 2005) which introduces a Dirichlet mixture distribution as a prior and alleviates the overfitting problem. We can expect to improve the transliteration accuracy by formulating the transliteration problem using a similar framework to these topic models.

In this paper, we formalize class-based transliteration based on language origins in the framework of topic models. We then propose the *latent semantic transliteration* model based on Dirichlet mixture (DM-LST). We show through experiments that it can significantly improve the transliteration performance by alleviating the overfitting issue.

Note that we tackle the task of *transliteration generation* in this paper, in contrast to *transliteration recognition*. A transliteration generation task is, given an input word $\boldsymbol{s}$ (such as "piaget"), the system is asked to generate from scratch the most probable transliterated word $\boldsymbol{t}$ (e.g., "ピアジェ *piaje*"). The transliteration recognition task, on the other hand, is to induce the most probable transliteration $\boldsymbol{t}^* \in T$ such that $\boldsymbol{t}^* = \arg\max_{\boldsymbol{t} \in T} P(\langle \boldsymbol{s}, \boldsymbol{t} \rangle)$ given the input word $\boldsymbol{s}$ and a pool of transliteration candidates T. We call $P(\langle \boldsymbol{s}, \boldsymbol{t} \rangle)$ *transliteration model* in this paper.

This model can be regarded as the hybrid of an unsupervised alignment technique for transliteration and class-based transliteration. Related researches for the former include (Ahmad and Kondrak, 2005), who estimate character-based error probabilities from query logs via the EM algorithm. For the latter, Llitjos and Black (2001) showed that source language origins may improve the pronunciation of proper nouns in text-to-speech systems.

The structure of this paper is as follows: we introduce the alpha-beta model(Brill and Moore, 2000) in Section 2, which is the most basic spelling-based transliteration model on which other models are based. In the following Section 3, we introduce and relate the joint source channel (JSC) model (Li et al., 2004) to the alpha-beta model. We describe the LCT model as an extension to the JSC model in Section 4. In Section 5, we propose the DM-LST model, and show the experimental results on transliteration generation in Section 6.

2 Alpha-Beta Model

In this section, we describe the alpha-beta model, which is one of the simplest spelling-based transliteration models. Though simple, the model has been shown to achieve better performance in tasks such as spelling correction (Brill and Moore, 2000), transliteration (Brill et al., 2001), and query alteration (Hagiwara and Suzuki, 2009).

The method directly models spelling-based re-writing probabilities of transliteration pairs. It is an extension to the normal edit distance, where the cost of operations (substitution, insertion, and deletion) is fixed to 1, and assigns a probability to a string edit operation of the form $s_i \rightarrow t_i$ (s_i and t_i are any substrings of length 0 to w). We call the unit operation of string re-writing $u_i = \langle s_i, t_i \rangle$ as transliteration unit (TU) as in (Li et al., 2004). The total transliteration probability of re-writing a word $\boldsymbol{s}$ to $\boldsymbol{t}$ is given by

$$P_{AB}(\langle \boldsymbol{s}, \boldsymbol{t} \rangle) = \max_{u_1 \ldots u_f} \prod_{i=1}^{f} P(u_i), \qquad (1)$$

where f is the number of TUs and $u_1 \ldots u_f$ is any sequence of TUs (e.g., "pi /ピ a /ア get /

ジェ") created by splitting up the input/output transliteration pair $\langle \boldsymbol{s}, \boldsymbol{t} \rangle$. The above equation can be interpreted as a problem of finding a TU sequence $u_1 \ldots u_f$ which maximizes the probability defined by the product of individual probabilities of independent TUs. After taking the logarithm of the both sides, and regarding $-\log P(u_i)$ as the cost of string substitution $s_i \rightarrow t_i$, the problem is equivalent to minimizing the sum of re-writing costs, and therefore can be efficiently solved by dynamic programming as done in the normal edit distance.

TU probabilities $P(u_i)$ are calculated from a training set of transliteration pairs. However, training sets usually lack alignment information specifying which characters in $\boldsymbol{s}$ corresponding which characters in $\boldsymbol{t}$. Brill and Moore (2000) resorted to heuristics to align same characters and to induce the alignment of string chunks. Hagiwara and Sekine (2011) converted Japanese Katakana sequences into Roman alphabets because their model also assumed that the strings s_i and t_i are expressed in the same alphabet system. Our method on the contrary, does not pose such assumption so that strings in different writing systems (such as Japanese Katakana and English alphabets, and Chinese characters and English alphabets, etc.) can be aligned without being converted to phonetic representation. For this reason, we cannot adopt algorithms (such as the one described in (Brill and Moore, 2000)) which heuristically infer alignment based on the correspondence of the same characters.

When applying this alpha-beta model, we computed TU probabilities by counting relative frequencies of all the alignment possibilities for a transliteration pair. For example, all the alignment possibilities for a pair of strings "abc" and "xy" are (a-x b-y c-ε), (a-x b-ε c-y), and (a-ε b-x c-y). By considering merging up to two adjacent aligned characters in the first alignment, one obtains the following five aligned string pairs: a-x, b-y, c-ε, ab-xy bc-y. Note that all the transliteration models described in this paper implicitly depend on the parameter w indicating the maximum length of character n-grams. We fixed $w = 3$ throughout this paper.

3 Joint Source Channel Model

The alpha-beta model described above has shortcomings that the character alignment is fixed based on heuristics, and it cannot capture the dependencies between TUs. One example of such dependencies is the phenomenon that the suffix "-ed" in English verbs following a voiced consonant is pronounced /d/, whereas the one followed by an unvoiced consonant is /t/. This section describes the JSC model(Li et al., 2004), which was independently proposed from the alpha-beta model. The JSC model is essentially equivalent to the alpha-beta model except: 1) it can also incorporate higher order of n-grams of TUs and 2) the TU statistics is taken not by fixing the heuristic initial alignment but by iteratively updating via an EM-like algorithm.

In the JSC model, the transliteration probability is defined by the n-gram probabilities of TUs $u_i = \langle s_i, t_i \rangle$ as follows:

$$P_{JSC}(\langle \boldsymbol{s}, \boldsymbol{t} \rangle) = \prod_{i=1}^{f} P(u_i | u_{i-n+1}, \ldots, u_{i-1}). \quad (2)$$

Again, f is the number of TUs. The TU n-gram probabilities $P(u_i | u_{i-n+1}, \ldots, u_{i-1})$ can be calculated by the following iterative updates similar to the EM algorithm:

1. Set the initial alignment randomly.
2. E-step: Take the TU n-gram statistics fixing the current alignment, and update the transliteration model.
3. M-step: Compute the alignment based on the current transliteration model. The alignment is inferred by dynamic programming similar to the alpha-beta model.
4. Iterate the E- and M- step until convergence.

Notice the alpha-beta model and the JSC model are both transliteration recognition models. In order to output a transliterated word $\boldsymbol{t}$ for a given input $\boldsymbol{s}$, we generated transliteration candidates with high probability using a stack

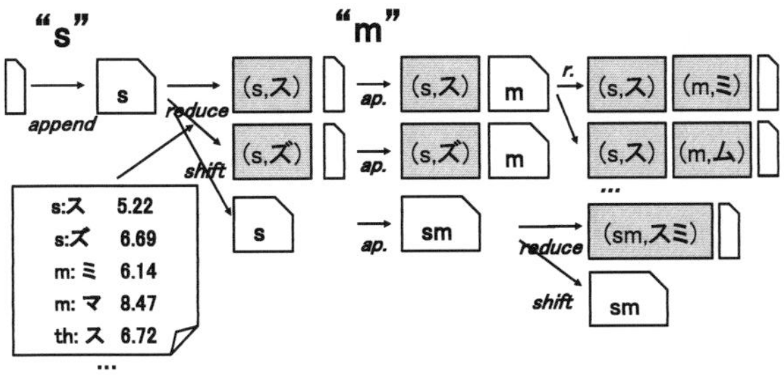

Figure 1: Overview of the stack decoder (generation of "スミス *sumisu*" from the input "smith")

decoder, whose overview is shown in Figure 1. One character in the input string $\boldsymbol{s}$ (which is "smith" in the figure) is given at a time, which is appended at the end of the last TUs for each candidate. (the *append* operation in the figure). Next, the last TU of each candidate is either *reduced* or *shifted*. When it is *reduced*, top R TUs with highest probabilities are generated and fixed referring to the TU table (shown in the bottom-left of the figure). In Figure 1, two candidates, namely ("s", "ス *su*") and ("s", "ズ *zu*") are generated after the character "s" is given. When the last TU is *shifted*, it remains unchanged and unfixed for further updates. Every time a single character is given, the transliteration probability is computed using Eq. 2 for each candidate, and all but the top-B candidates with highest probabilities are discarded. The reduce width R and the beam width B were determined using the determined using development sets, as mentioned in Section 6.

4 Latent Class Transliteration Model

As mentioned in Section 1, the alpha-beta model and the JSC model build a single transliteration model which is simply the monolithic average of training set statistics, failing to capture the difference in the source language origins. Li et al. (2004) address this issue by defining classes c, i.e., the factors such as source language origins, gender, and first/last names, etc. which affect the transliteration probability. The authors then propose the class transliteration model which gives the probability of $\boldsymbol{s} \rightarrow \boldsymbol{t}$ as follows:

$$P_{LI}(\boldsymbol{t}|\boldsymbol{s}) = \sum_{c} P(\boldsymbol{t}, c|\boldsymbol{s}) = \sum_{c} P(c|\boldsymbol{s}) P(\boldsymbol{t}|c, \boldsymbol{s}) \quad (3)$$

However, this model requires a training set explicitly tagged with the classes. Instead of assigning an explicit class c to each transliterated pair, Hagiwara and Sekine (2011) introduce a random variable z which indicates implicit classes and conditional TU probability $P(u_i|z)$. The latent class transliteration (LCT) model is then defined as[1]:

$$P_{\mathrm{LCT}}(\langle \boldsymbol{s}, \boldsymbol{t} \rangle) = \sum_{z=1}^{K} P(z) \prod_{i=1}^{f} P(u_i|z) \quad (4)$$

where K is the number of the latent classes. The latent classes z correspond to classes such as the language origins and genders mentioned above, shared by sets of transliterated pairs with similar re-writing characteristics. The classes z are not directly observable from the training set, but can be induced by maximizing the training set likelihood via the EM algorithm as follows.

$$\textbf{Parameters:} \quad P(z = k) = \pi_k, \ P(u_i|z) \quad (5)$$

$$\textbf{E-Step:} \ \gamma_{nk} = \frac{\pi_k P(\langle \boldsymbol{s}_n, \boldsymbol{t}_n \rangle | z = k)}{\sum_{k'=1}^{K} \pi_{k'} P(\langle \boldsymbol{s}_n, \boldsymbol{t}_n \rangle | z = k')}, \quad (6)$$

$$P(\langle \boldsymbol{s}_n, \boldsymbol{t}_n \rangle | z) = \max_{u_1..u_f} \prod_{i=1}^{f_n} P(u_i|z) \quad (7)$$

$$\textbf{M-Step:} \quad \pi_k^{new} \propto \sum_{n=1}^{N} \gamma_{nk}, \quad (8)$$

$$P(u_i|z = k)^{new} = \frac{1}{N_k} \sum_{n=1}^{N} \gamma_{nk} \frac{f_n(u_i)}{f_n} \quad (9)$$

where $N_k = \sum_n \gamma_{nk}$. Here, $\langle \boldsymbol{s}_n, \boldsymbol{t}_n \rangle$ is the n-th transliterated pair in the training set, and f_n and $f_n(u_i)$ indicate how many TUs there are in total in the n-th transliterated pair, and how many times the TU u_i appeared in it, respectively. As done in the JSC model, we update the alignment in the training set before the E-Step for each iteration. Thus f_n takes different values

[1]Note that this LCT model is formalized by introducing a latent variable to the transliteration generative probability $P(\langle \boldsymbol{s}, \boldsymbol{t} \rangle)$ as in the JSC model, not to $P(\boldsymbol{t}|\boldsymbol{s})$.

from iteration to iteration in general. Furthermore, since the alignment is updated based on $P(u_i|z)$ for each $z = k$, M different alignment candidates are retained for each transliterated pairs, which makes the value of f_n dependent on k, i.e., f_n^k. We initialize $P(z = k) = 1/M$ to and $P(u_i|z) = P_{AB}(u) + \varepsilon$, that is, the TU probability induced by the alpha-beta algorithm plus some random noise ε.

Considering a TU as a word, and a transliteration pair as a document consisting of a word sequence, this LCT model defines the transliteration probability as the mixture of multinomials defined over TUs. This can be formulated by unigram mixture (Nigam et al., 2000), which is a topic model over documents. This follows a generation story where documents (i.e., transliterated pairs) are generated firstly by choosing a class z by $P(z)$ and then by generating a word (i.e., TU) by $P(u_i|z)$. Nevertheless, as mentioned in Section 1, since this model trains the parameters based on the maximum likelihood estimation over multinomials, it is vulnerable to noise in the training set, thus prone to overfit the data.

5 Latent Semantic Transliteration Model based on Dirichlet Mixture

We propose the latent semantic transliteration model based on Dirichlet mixture (DM-LST), which is an extension to the LCT model based on unigram mixture. This model enables to prevent multinomials from being exceedingly biased towards the given data, still being able to model the transliteration generation by a mixture of multiple latent classes, by introducing Dirichlet mixture as a prior to TU multinomials. The compound distribution of multinomials when their parameters are given by Dirichlet mixtures is given by the Polya mixture distribution(Yamamoto and Sadamitsu, 2005):

$$P_{DM}(\langle \boldsymbol{s}, \boldsymbol{t} \rangle) \tag{10}$$

$$= \int P_{Mul}(\langle \boldsymbol{s}, \boldsymbol{t} \rangle; \boldsymbol{p}) P_{DM}(\boldsymbol{p}; \boldsymbol{\lambda}, \boldsymbol{\alpha}_1^K) d\boldsymbol{p}$$

$$\propto \sum_{k=1}^{K} \lambda_k P_{Polya}(\langle \boldsymbol{s}, \boldsymbol{t} \rangle; \boldsymbol{\alpha}_1^K) \tag{11}$$

$$= \sum_{k=1}^{K} \lambda_k \frac{\Gamma(\alpha_k)}{\Gamma(\alpha_k + f)} \prod_{i=1}^{f} \frac{\Gamma(f(u_i) + \alpha_{ku_i})}{\Gamma(\alpha_{ku_i})}$$

where $P_{Mul}(*; \boldsymbol{p})$ is multinomial with the parameter $\boldsymbol{p}$. P_{DM} is Dirichlet mixture, which is a mixture (with co-efficients $\lambda_1, ..., \lambda_K$) of K Dirichlet distributions with parameters $\alpha_1^K = (\boldsymbol{\alpha}_1, \boldsymbol{\alpha}_2, ..., \boldsymbol{\alpha}_K)$.

The model parameters can be induced by the following EM algorithm. Notice that we adopted a fast induction algorithm which extends an induction method using leaving-one-out to mixture distributions(Yamamoto et al., 2003).

Parameters: $\boldsymbol{\lambda} = (\lambda_1, ..., \lambda_K)$, (12)

$$\boldsymbol{\alpha}_1^K = (\boldsymbol{\alpha}_1, \boldsymbol{\alpha}_2, ..., \boldsymbol{\alpha}_K) \tag{13}$$

E-Step: $$\eta_{nk} = \frac{\lambda_k P_{Polya}(\langle \boldsymbol{s}_n, \boldsymbol{t}_n \rangle; \boldsymbol{\alpha}_k)}{\sum_{k'} \lambda_{k'} P_{Polya}(\langle \boldsymbol{s}_n, \boldsymbol{t}_n \rangle; \boldsymbol{\alpha}_{k'})} \tag{14}$$

M-Step: $$\lambda_k^{new} \propto \sum_{n=1}^{N} \eta_{nk} \tag{15}$$

$$\alpha_{ku}^{new} = \alpha_{ku} \frac{\sum_n \eta_{nk} \{f_n(u)/(f_n(u) - 1 + \alpha_{ku})\}}{\sum_n \eta_{nk} \{f_n/(f_n - 1 + \alpha_k)\}} \tag{16}$$

The prediction distribution when a single TU u is the input is given $P_{DM}(u) = \sum_{k=1}^{K} \lambda_k \alpha_{ku} / \alpha_k$. We therefore updated the alignment in the training corpus, as done in the JSC model updates, based on the probability proportional to α_{ku}/α_k for each k before every M-Step. The parameters are initially set to $\lambda_k = 1/K$, $\alpha_{ku} = P_{AB}(u) + \varepsilon$, as explained in the previous section.

Since neither LCT nor DM-LST is a transliteration generation model, we firstly generated transliteration candidates T by using the JSC model and the stack decoder (Section 3) as a baseline, then re-ranked the candidates using the probabilities given by LCT (Eq. 4 or DM-LST (Eq. 11), generating the re-ranked list of transliterated outputs. Because the parameters trained by the EM algorithm differ depending on the initial values, we trained 10 models $P^1_{DM}, ..., P^{10}_{DM}$ using the same training data and random initial values and computed the average $\frac{1}{10}\sum_{j=1}^{10} P^j_{DM}(\langle \boldsymbol{s}, \boldsymbol{t} \rangle)$ to be used as the final transliteration model.

It is worth mentioning that another topic model, namely latent Dirichlet allocation (LDA) (Blei et al., 2003), assumes that words in a document can be generated from different topics from each other. This assumption corresponds to the notion that TUs in a single transliterated pairs can be generated from different source languages, which is presumably a wrong assumption for transliteration tasks, probably except for compound-like words with mixed origins such as "naïveness". In fact, we confirmed through a preliminary experiment that LDA does not improve the transliteration performance over the baseline.

6 Experiments

6.1 Evaluation

In this section, we compare the following models: alpha-beta (AB), joint source channel (JSC), latent class transliteration (LCT), and latent semantic transliteration based on Dirichlet mixture (DM-LST).

For the performance evaluation, we used three language pairs, namely, English-Japanese (En-Ja), English-Chinese (En-Ch), and English-Korean (En-Ko), from the transliteration shared task at NEWS 2009 (Li et al., 2009a; Li et al., 2009b). The size of each training/test set is shown in the first column of Table 1. In general, $\boldsymbol{r}_n$, a set of one or more reference transliterated words, is associated with the n-th input $\boldsymbol{s}_n$ in the training/test corpus. Let $c_{n,i}, c_{n,2}, ...$ be the output of the transliteration system, i.e., the candidates with highest probabilities assigned by the transliteration model being evaluated. We used the following three performance measures:

- **ACC** (averaged Top-1 accuracy): For every $\langle \boldsymbol{s}_n, \boldsymbol{r}_n \rangle$, let a_n be $a_n = 1$ if the candidate with the highest probability $c_{n,1}$ is contained in the reference set $\boldsymbol{r}_n$ and $a_n = 0$ otherwise. ACC is then calculated as $ACC\frac{1}{N}\sum_{i=1}^{N} s_n$.

- **MFS** (mean F score): Let the reference transliterated word closest to the top-1 candidate $c_n, 1$ be $r^*_n = \arg\min_{r_{n,j} \in \boldsymbol{r}_n} ED(c_{n,1}, r_{n,j})$, where ED is the edit distance. The F-score of the top candidate $c_{n,1}$ for the n-th input $\boldsymbol{s}_n$ is then given by:

$$\begin{aligned} P_n &= LSC(c_{n,1}, r^*_n)/|c_{n,1}| & (17) \\ R_n &= LCS(c_{n,1}, r^*_n)/|r^*_n| & (18) \\ F_n &= 2R_iP_i/(R_i + P_i), & (19) \end{aligned}$$

  where $|x|$ is the length of string x, and $LCS(x, y)$ is the length of the longest common subsequence of x and y. Edit distance, lengths of strings, and LCS are measured in Unicode characters. Finally, MFS is defined as $MFS = \frac{1}{N}\sum_{i=1}^{N} F_n$.

- **MRR** (mean reciprocal rank): Of the ranked candidates $c_{n,1}, c_{n,2}, ...$, let the highest ranked one which is also included in the reference set $\boldsymbol{r}_n$ be $c_{n,j}$. We then define reciprocal rank $RR_n = 1/j$. If none of the candidates are in the reference, $RR_n = 0$. MRR is then defined by $MRR = \frac{1}{N}\sum_{n=1}^{N} RR_n$.

We used Kneser-Nay smoothing to smooth the TU probabilities for LCT. The number of EM iterations is fixed to 15 for all the models, based on the result of preliminary experiments.

The reduce width R and the beam width B for the stack decoder are fixed to $R = 8$ and $B = 32$, because the transliteration generation performance increased very little beyond these widths based on the experiment using the development set. We also optimized M, i.e., the number of latent classes for LCT and DM-LST, for each language pair and model in the same way based on the development set.

Table 1: Performance comparison of transliteration models

Language pair	Model	ACC	MFS	MRR
En-Ja	AB	0.293	0.755	0.378
Train: 23,225	JSC	0.326	0.770	0.428
Test: 1,489	LCT	0.345	0.768	0.437
	DM-LST	**0.349**	**0.776**	**0.444**
En-Ch	AB	0.358	0.741	0.471
Train: 31,961	JSC	0.417	0.761	0.527
Test: 2,896	LCT	0.430	0.764	0.532
	DM-LST	**0.445**	**0.770**	**0.546**
En-Ko	AB	0.145	0.537	0.211
Train: 4,785	JSC	0.151	0.543	0.221
Test: 989	LCT	0.079	0.483	0.167
	DM-LST	**0.174**	**0.556**	**0.237**

6.2 Results

We compared the performance of each transliteration model in Table 1. For the language pairs En-Ja and En-Ch, all the performance increase in the order of AB $<$ JSC $<$ LCT $<$ DM-LST, showing the superiority our proposed method. For the language pair En-Ko, the performance for LCT re-ranking considerably decreases compared to JSC. We suspect this is due to the relatively small number of training set, which caused the excessive fitting to the data. We also found out that the optimal value of M which maximizes the performance of DM-LST is equal to or smaller than that of LCT. This goes along with the findings (Yamamoto and Sadamitsu, 2005) that Dirichlet mixture often achieves better language model perplexity with smaller dimensionality compared to other models.

Specific examples in the En-Ja test set whose transliteration is improved by the proposed methods include "dijon ／ディジョン *dijon*" and "goldenberg ／ゴールデンバーグ *gōrudenbāgu*". Conventional methods, including LCT, suggested "ディヨン *diyon*" and "ゴールデンベルグ *gōrudenberugu*", meaning that the transliteration model is affected and biased towards non-English pronunciation. The proposed method can retain the major class of transliteration characteristics (which is English in this case) and can deal with multiple language origins depending on transliteration pairs at the same time.

This trend can be also confirmed in other language pairs, En-Ch and En-Ko. In En-Ch, the transliterated words of "covell" and "netherwood" are improved " "科夫尔 *kefuer* →科维尔 *keweier*" and "内特赫伍德 *neitehewude* →内瑟伍德 *neisewude*", respectively. in En-Ko, the transliterated word of "darling" is improved "다르링 *dareuling*" → "달링 *dalling*".

We also observed that "gutheim / 古特海姆 *gutehaimu* in En-Ch and martina / 마르티나 *mareutina* in En-Ko are correctly translated by the proposed method, even though they do not have the English origin. Generally speaking, however, how these non-English words are pronounced depend on the context, as "charles" has different pronunciation in English and in French, with the soft "sh" sound at the beginning. We need external clues to disambiguate such transliteration, such as context information and/or Web statistics.

7 Conclusion

In this paper, we proposed the latent semantic transliteration model based on Dirichlet mixture (DM-LST) as the extension to the latent class transliteration model. The experimental results showed the superior transliteration performance over the conventional methods, since DM-LST can alleviate the overfitting problem and can capture multiple language origins. One drawback is that it cannot deal with dependencies of higher order of TU n-grams than bigrams. How to incorporate these dependencies into the latent transliteration models is the future work.

References

Farooq Ahmad and Grzegorz Kondrak. 2005. Learning a spelling error model from search query logs. In *Proc. of EMNLP-2005*, pages 955–962.

David M. Blei, Andrew Y. Ng, and Michael I. Jordan. 2003. Latent dirichlet allocation. *Journal of Machine Learning Research*, 3:993–1022.

Eric Brill and Robert C. Moore. 2000. An improved error model for noisy channel spelling. In *Proc. ACL-2000*, pages 286–293.

Eric Brill, Gary Kacmarcik, and Chris Brockett. 2001. Automatically harvesting katakana-english term pairs from search engine query logs. In *Proc. NLPRS-2001*, pages 393–399.

Masato Hagiwara and Satoshi Sekine. 2011. Latent class transliteration based on source language origin. In *Proc. of ACL-HLT 2011*, pages 53–57.

Masato Hagiwara and Hisami Suzuki. 2009. Japanese query alteration based on semantic similarity. In *Proc. of NAACL-2009*, page 191.

Kevin Knight and Graehl Jonathan. 1998. Machine transliteration. *Computational Linguistics*, 24:599–612.

Haizhou Li, Zhang Min, and Su Jian. 2004. A joint source-channel model for machine transliteration. In *Proc. of ACL 2004*, pages 159–166.

Haizhou Li, Khe Chai Sum, Jin-Shea Kuo, and Minghui Dong. 2007. Semantic transliteration of personal names. In *Proc. of ACL 2007*, pages 120–127.

Haizhou Li, A Kumaran, Vladimir Pervouchine, and Min Zhang. 2009a. Report of news 2009 machine transliteration shared task. In *Proc. of the 2009 Named Entities Workshop*, pages 1–18.

Haizhou Li, A Kumaran, Min Zhang, and Vladimir Pervouchine. 2009b. Whitepaper of news 2009 machine transliteration shared task. In *Proc. of the 2009 Named Entities Workshop*, pages 19–26.

Ariadna Font Llitjos and Alan W. Black. 2001. Knowledge of language origin improves pronunciation accuracy. In *Proc. of Eurospeech*, pages 1919–1922.

Kamal Nigam, Andrew Kachites McCallum, Sebastian Thrun, and Tom Mitchell. 2000. Text classification from labeled and unlabeled documents using em. *Machine Learning*, 39(2):103–134.

K. Sjölander, K. Karplus, M. Brown, R. Hunghey, A. Krogh, I.S. Mian, and D. Haussler. 1996. Dirichlet mixtures:a method for improved detection of weak but significant protein sequence homology. *Computer Applications in the Biosciences*, 12(4):327–345.

Mikio Yamamoto and Kugatsu Sadamitsu. 2005. Dirichlet mixtures in text modeling. *CS Technical Report*, CS-TR-05-1.

Mikio Yamamoto, Kugatsu Sadamitsu, and Takuya Mishina. 2003. Context modeling using dirichlet mixtures and its applications to language models (in japnaese). *IPSJ*, 2003-SLP-48:29–34.

Automatically generated NE tagged corpora for English and Hungarian

Dávid Márk Nemeskey
Research Institute for
Computer Science and Automation
Hungarian Academy of Sciences
H-1111 Kende utca 13-17, Budapest
nemeskey.david@sztaki.mta.hu

Eszter Simon
Research Institute for Linguistics
Hungarian Academy of Sciences
H-1068 Benczúr utca 33, Budapest
simon.eszter@nytud.mta.hu

Abstract

Supervised Named Entity Recognizers require large amounts of annotated text. Since manual annotation is a highly costly procedure, reducing the annotation cost is essential. We present a fully automatic method to build NE annotated corpora from Wikipedia. In contrast to recent work, we apply a new method, which maps the DBpedia classes into CoNLL NE types. Since our method is mainly language-independent, we used it to generate corpora for English and Hungarian. The corpora are freely available.

1 Introduction

Named Entity Recognition (NER), the task of identifying Named Entities (NEs) in unstructured texts and classifying them into pre-selected classes, is one of the most important subtasks in many NLP tasks, such as information retrieval, information extraction or machine translation. The NER task was introduced with the 6th Message Understanding Conference (MUC) in 1995 (Grishman and Sundheim, 1996). In MUC shared tasks the NER consists of three subtasks: entity names, temporal and number expressions. Although there is a general agreement in the NER community about the inclusion of temporal expressions and some numerical expressions, the most studied types are names of persons, locations and organizations. The fourth type, called "miscellaneous", was introduced in the CoNLL NER tasks in 2002 (Tjong Kim Sang, 2002) and 2003 (Tjong Kim Sang and De Meulder, 2003), and includes proper names falling outside the three classic types. Since then, MUC and CoNLL datasets and annotation schemes have been the major standards applied in the field of NER.

The standard datasets are highly domain-specific (mostly newswire) and are restricted in size. Researchers attempting to merge these datasets to get a bigger training corpus are faced with the problem of combining different tagsets and annotation schemes. Manually annotating large amounts of text with linguistic information is a time-consuming, highly skilled and delicate job, but large, accurately annotated corpora are essential for building robust supervised machine learning NER systems. Therefore, reducing the annotation cost is a key challenge.

One approach is to generate the resources automatically, another one is to use collaborative annotation and/or collaboratively constructed resources, such as Wikipedia, Wiktionary, Linked Open Data, or DBpedia. In this paper we combine these approaches by automatically generating freely available NE tagged corpora from Wikipedia.

The paper is structured as follows. In Section 2 we give an overview of related work. Section 3 contains a description of our method, and Section 4 shows how it is applied to Hungarian. The corpus format is described in Section 5. In Section 6 we present experiments and results on the newly generated datasets. Section 7 concludes the paper with a summary.

2 Wikipedia and NER

Wikipedia (WP, see `http://wikipedia.org`), a free multilingual Internet encyclopedia, written collaboratively by volunteers, is a goldmine of information: at the time of writing, WP contains about 21 million interlinked articles. Of these, 3,903,467 are English, and 212,120 are Hungarian. WP has been applied to several NLP tasks such as word sense disambiguation, ontology and thesaurus building, and question answering (see Medelyan et al. (2009) for a survey). It is recognized as one of the largest available collections of entities, and also as a resource that can improve the accuracy of NER. The most obvious utilization of WP for NER is extracting gazetteers containing person names, locations or organizations (e.g. Toral and Muñoz (2006)). Creating dictionaries of entities is also a common step of NE disambiguation (Bunescu and Pasca, 2006; Cucerzan, 2007). Both supervised and unsupervised NER systems use such lists, see e.g. Nadeau et al. (2006) The knowledge embodied in WP may also be incorporated in NER learning as features, e.g. Kazama and Torisawa (2007) showed that automatic extraction of category labels from WP improves the accuracy of a supervised NE tagger.

Another approach to improve NER with WP is the automatic creation of training data. Richman and Schone (2008) built corpora for less commonly taught languages annotated with NE tags. They used the inherent category structure of WP to determine the NE type of a proposed entity. Nothman et al. (2008) used a similar method to create a NE annotated text in English. They transformed the WP links into NE annotations by classifying the target articles into standard entity classes. Their approach to classification is based primarily on category head nouns and the opening sentences of articles where definitions are often given.

Our approach to recognize and classify NEs in corpora generated from WP was to map the DBpedia ontology classes to standard NE tags and assign these to WP entities (see more details in Section 3.1). Except for the Semantically Annotated Snapshot of the English WP (SASWP) (Zaragoza et al., 2007), no such automatically built corpora are freely available. SASWP provides a wide range of linguistic information: POS tags, dependency labels, WordNet super senses and NE annotation according to WSJ and CoNLL tagsets. Even though the SASWP NEs were tagged by the best available open source taggers, the tags provided here, being based on the manual judgement of thousands of WP volunteers, are more reliable. Given the huge number of WP articles we can build sufficiently large corpora for less resourced languages as well, as our method is largely language-independent. We demonstrate this on Hungarian, a highly agglutinative language, with free word order and other typological characteristics detailed later in Section 4. There are smaller, manually annotated CoNLL-style datasets, but the one presented here is the first automatically NE annotated corpus for Hungarian.

3 Creating the English Corpus

Our goal is to create a large NE annotated corpus, automatically generated from WP articles. We followed a similar path to Nothman et al. (2008) and broke down the process into four steps:

1. Classify WP articles into entity classes.
2. Parse WP and split articles into sentences.
3. Label named entities in the text.
4. Select the sentences for inclusion in the corpus.

In this section, we describe how these steps were implemented. This section explains the general approach and its execution for English; Section 4 describes how the idea is adapted to Hungarian.

3.1 Articles as Entities

Many authors, such as Kazama and Torisawa (2007) and Nothman et al. (2008) used semi-supervised methods based on WP categories and text to classify articles into NE types. To avoid the inevitable classification errors, we obtain entity type information from the DBpedia knowledge base (Bizer et al., 2009), which presents type, properties, home pages, etc. information about pages in WP in structured form. With DBpedia we have high precision information about entity types at the expense of recall: of the 3,903,467 English WP pages, 1,470,293 are covered by DBpedia (as of 18 March, 2012).

The types in DBpedia are organized into a class hierarchy, available as an OWL[1] ontology containing 320 frequent entity categories, arranged into a taxonomy under the base class `owl:Thing`.

[1] http://www.w3.org/TR/owl-ref/

Most of the classes belong to the 6 largest sub-hierarchies: `Person`, `Organisation`, `Event`, `Place`, `Species` and `Work`. The taxonomy is rather flat: the top level contains 44 classes and there are several nodes with a branching factor of 20.

The type of entities is extracted automatically from WP categories. However, the mapping between WP categories and classes in the DBpedia ontology is manually defined. This, together with the fact that the existence of the reference ontology prevents the proliferation of categories observable in WP (Bizer et al., 2009), ensures that type information in DBpedia can be considered gold quality.

From the available NER annotation standards we elected to use the CoNLL (Tjong Kim Sang and De Meulder, 2003) NE types. It is not difficult to see the parallels between the DBpedia sub-hierarchies `Person`, `Organisation` and `Place` and the CoNLL NE types `PER`, `ORG` and `LOC`. The fourth category, `MISC` is more elusive; according to the CoNLL NER annotation guide[2], the sub-hierarchies `Event` and `Work` belong to this category, as well as various other classes outside the main hierarchies.

While the correspondence described above holds for most classes in the sub-hierarchies, there are some exceptions. For instance, the class `SportsLeague` is part of the `Organisation` sub-hierarchy, but according to the CoNLL annotation scheme, they should be tagged as `MISC`. To avoid misclassification, we created a file of DBpedia class–NE category mappings. Whenever an entity is evaluated, we look up its class and the ancestors of its class, and assign to it the category of the class that matches it most closely. If no match is found, the entity is tagged with `O`.

As of version 3.7, the DBpedia ontology allows multiple superclasses, making a directed acyclic graph[3]. Since selecting the right superclass, and hence, CoNLL tag, for classes with more than one parent cannot be reliably done automatically, the class-to-category mapping had to be determined manually. The only such class in version 3.7, `Library`, can be traced back to both `Place` and `Organisation`; its CoNLL tag is `LOC`. Using the mapping thus created, we compile a list that contains all entities in DBpedia tagged with the appropriate CoNLL category.

We note here that our method can be trivially modified to work with any tagset compatible with the DBpedia ontology (indeed, the DBpedia classes define a NE tagset themselves), but we leave the exploration of these possibilities for future work.

3.2 Parsing Wikipedia

WP is a rich source of information; in addition to the article text, a huge amount of data is embedded in infoboxes, templates, and the category structure. Our task requires only the links between the articles and the article text. In addition to in-article links, our method takes advantage of the redirect and interlanguage links, available as SQL dumps. The English corpus is based on the WP snapshot as of January 15, 2011. The XML files were parsed by the mwlib parser[4], the raw text was tokenized by a modified version of the Punkt sentence and word tokenizers (Kiss and Strunk, 2002). For lemmatization we used the Wordnet Lemmatizer in NLTK (Bird et al., 2009), and for part-of-speech tagging the HunPOS tagger (Halácsy et al., 2007).

3.3 Named Entity Labeling

In order to automatically prepare sentences where NEs are accurately tagged, two tasks need to be performed: identifying entities in the sentence and tagging them with the correct tag. Sentences for which accurate tagging could not be accomplished must be removed from the corpus. Our approach is based on the work of Nothman et al. (2008). The WP cross-references found in the article text are used to identify entities. We assume that individual WP articles describe NEs. A link to an article can then be perceived as a mapping that identifies its anchor text with a particular NE.

The discovered entities are tagged with the CoNLL label assigned to them in the entity list extracted from DBpedia. If the link target is not in the entity list, or the link points to a disambiguation page, we cannot determine the type of the entity, and tag it as UNK for subsequent removal from the corpus. Links to redirect pages are resolved to point instead to the redirect target, after which they are han-

[2]http://www.cnts.ua.ac.be/conll2003/ner/annotation.txt

[3]http://blog.dbpedia.org/2011/09/11/dbpedia-37-released-including-15-localized-editions

[4]http://code.pediapress.com

dled as regular cross-references. Finally, sentences with UNK links in them are removed from the corpus.

The following sub-sections describe how the method explained above can be improved to increase precision, sentence coverage and to account for peculiarities in the English orthography and the CoNLL guidelines.

3.3.1 Non-entity Links

Strictly speaking, our original assumption of equating WP articles with NEs is not valid: many pages describe common nouns (Book, Aircraft), calendar-related concepts (March 15, 2007), or other concepts that fall outside the scope of NER. To increase sentence coverage, we modified the algorithm to prevent it from misclassifying links to these pages as unknown entities and discarding the sentence.

Common noun links are filtered by POS tags; if a link contains no `NNP`s, it is ignored.

Time expression links require special attention, because dates and months are often linked to the respective WP pages. We circumvented this problem by compiling a list of calendar-related pages and adding them to the main entity list tagged with the CoNLL category `O`.

Lowercase links for entities referred to by common nouns, such as *republic* to *Roman Republic* are not considered NEs and are ignored.

3.3.2 Unmarked Entities

In a WP article, typically only the first occurrence of a particular entity is linked to the corresponding page. Subsequent mentions are unmarked and often incomplete – e.g. family names are used instead of full names. To account for such mentions, we apply Nothman's (2008) solution. For each page, we maintain a list of entities discovered in the page so far and try to associate capitalized words in the article text with these entities. We augment the list with the aliases of every entity, such as titles of redirect pages that target it, the first and last names in case of a `PER` entity and any numbers in the name. If the current page is a NE, the title and its aliases are added to the list as well; moreover, as WP usually includes the original name of foreign entities in the article text, localized versions of the title are also added to the list as aliases. Nothman's solution used a trie to store the entity list, while we use a set, with more alias types than what he used. We expect more precise tagging from our slightly more rigorous solution.

3.3.3 Special Cases

Derived words According to the CoNLL guidelines, words derived from NEs are tagged as `MISC`. We complied with this rule by tagging each entity whose head is not a noun, as well as when the link's anchor text is not contained in the entity's name, as `MISC`. The most prominent example for such entities are nationalities, which can be linked to their home country, a `LOC`; e.g. *Turkish* to *Turkey*. Our solution assigns the correct tag to these entities.

First word in a sentence As first words are always capitalized, labeling them is difficult if they are unlinked and not contained in the entity alias set. We base the decision on the POS tag of the first word: if it is `NNP`, we tag it as `UNK`; otherwise, `O`.

Reference cleansing Page titles and anchor texts may contain more than just the entity name. Personal titles are part of the entity name in WP, but not in CoNLL, and punctuation marks around the entity may become part of the link by mistake. We tag all punctuation marks after the entity name as `O`.

To handle personal titles, we extracted a list from the WP page *List of titles*, which contains titles in many languages. We manually removed all titles that also function as given names, such as *Regina*. If a link to a `PER` or `UNK` entity, or an unlinked entity starts with, or consists solely of a title in the list, we tag the words that make up the title as `O`.

Incidental capitalization Various non-`NNP` words in English are capitalized: names of months, the pronoun *I*, and non-entity acronyms such as *RSVP*. While the latter two types are unlikely to appear in WP text, we assembled a list of these words and tag them as `O` unless they are part of the alias set.

3.4 Sentence Filtering

As mentioned above, sentences with words tagged as `UNK` are discarded. Furthermore, there are many incomplete sentences in the WP text: image captions, enumerations items, contents of table cells, etc. On the one hand, these sentence fragments may be of too low quality to be of any use in the traditional NER task. On the other hand, they could prove to be invaluable when training a NER tagger for User Generated Content, which is known to be noisy and fragmented. As a compromise we included these fragments in the corpus, but labelled them as "low quality", so that users of the corpus can decide whether they want to use them or not. A sentence is labelled as such if it either lacks a punctuation mark at the end, or it contains no finite verb.

4 Creating the Hungarian Corpus

The procedure described in the previous section was used to generate the Hungarian corpus as well. However, typological differences posed several problems. In this section we describe the differences between the two languages related to labeling NEs, and the changes they prompted in the method.

4.1 Parsing the Hungarian Wikipedia

Although Hungarian is reckoned to be a less resourced language, and it is not supported in NLTK, several high quality language processing tools have been developed for Hungarian in recent years. For tokenization and sentence segmentation we used an in-house statistical tool tailored for Hungarian. It has been trained on the largest manually annotated Hungarian corpus (Csendes et al., 2004), and it handles the peculiarities of Hungarian orthography, such as the periods placed after numbers in date expressions. Lemmatization was performed by HunMorph (Trón et al., 2005) and HunDisambig, an in-house disambiguator to select the right analysis based on the word context.

For the most part Hungarian expresses grammatical elements within a word form using affixes. HunMorph outputs KR-codes (Kornai et al., 2004), which, in addition to the POS category, also include inflectional information, making it much better suited to agglutinative languages than Penn Treebank POS tags. One shortcoming of the KR-code is that it does not differentiate between common and proper nouns. Since in Hungarian only proper nouns are capitalized, we can usually decide whether a noun is proper based on the initial letter. However, this rule can not be used if the noun is at the beginning of a sentence, so sentences that begin with nouns have been removed from the corpus.

4.2 Named Entity Labeling in Hungarian

For well-resourced languages, DBpedia has internationalized chapters, but not for Hungarian. Instead, the Hungarian entity list comprises of the pages in the English list that have their equivalents in the Hungarian WP. Two consequences follow. First, in order to identify which pages denote entities in the Hungarian WP, an additional step is required, in which the Hungarian equivalents of the English pages are added to the entity list. The English titles are retained because (due to the medium size of the Hungarian WP) in-article links sometimes point to English articles.

Second, entities without a page in the English WP are absent from the entity list. This gives rise to two potential problems. One is that compared to English, the list is relatively shorter: the entity/page ratio is 12.12%, as opposed to the 37.66% of the English WP. The other, since mostly Hungarian people, places and organizations are missing, a NER tagger that takes the surface forms of words into account might be mislead as to the language model of entity names. To overcome these problems, the list has to be extended with Hungarian entity pages that do not have a corresponding English page. We leave this for future work.

To annotate our corpus with NE tags, we chose to follow the annotation guidelines of the largest human-annotated NER corpus for Hungarian, the Szeged NER corpus (Szarvas et al., 2006). It is similar to CoNLL standards: contains newswire texts, comprises ca. 200,000 tokens, and is annotated with NE class labels in line with the CoNLL annotation scheme. However, the convention of what constitutes a NE is slightly different for Hungarian.

4.2.1 Special cases

The Szeged NER guideline relies heavily on the rules of capitalization to decide which words should be marked as NEs. The following concepts are not

train	test	precision	recall	F-measure
Szeged NER	Szeged NER	94.50	94.35	94.43
huwiki	huwiki	90.64	88.91	89.76
huwiki	Szeged NER	63.08	70.46	66.57
Szeged NER with wikilists	Szeged NER	95.48	95.48	95.48
Szeged NER with wikitags	Szeged NER	95.38	94.92	95.15

Table 1: Hungarian results.

proper nouns in Hungarian, and thus are not considered as NEs: names of languages, nationalities, religions, political ideologies; adjectives derived from NEs; names of months, days, holidays; names of special events and wars.

There is another special case in Hungarian: unlike in English, the number of compound words is quite large, and NEs can also be subject to compounding. In this case the common noun following the NE is joined with a hyphen, so they constitute one token. However, the joint common noun can modify the original sense of NE, depending on the semantics of the common noun. For example in the compound *Nobel-díj* ['Nobel Prize'] the common noun changes the labeling from `PER` to `MISC`, while in the case of the compound *WorldCom-botrány* ['WorldCom scandal'] the NE tag changes from `ORG` to `O`. The solution to this problem is not obvious, and needs more investigation.

5 Data Description

The corpora are available under the Creative Commons Attribution-Sharealike 3.0 Unported License (CC-BY-SA), the same license under which the text of WP is released. The data files can be freely downloaded from `http://hlt.sztaki.hu`. The corpora will also be distributed through the META-SHARE network, which is an open, distributed facility for exchanging and sharing resources, and is one of the lines of action of META-NET, a Network of Excellence funded by the European Commission.

The files are in multitag format. Content lines are tab separated; there is one column for the tokens plus one column per tagset. Sentence boundaries are marked by empty lines. The linguistic features include the lemmatized form of the word and its POS tag. Two NE tags are included with each word: the most specific DBpedia category it belongs to and the CoNLL NE tag. While the NE tags can be considered as a "silver standard", the linguistic features are provided on a "best-effort" basis.

6 Evaluation

Having the obvious advantages, an automatically generated corpus can not serve as a gold standard dataset. Then what can we do with silver standard corpora? They can be very useful for improving NER in several ways: (a) for less resourced languages, they can serve as training corpora in lieu of gold standard datasets; (b) they can serve as supplementary or independent training sets for domains differing from newswire; (c) they can be sources of huge entity lists, and (d) feature extraction.

To evaluate our corpora we used a maximum entropy NE tagger (Varga and Simon, 2007), which was originally developed for labeling NEs in Hungarian texts, but can be tuned for different languages as well. Corpus-specific features (e.g. NP chunks, WP links) were removed to get better comparability, so the feature set consists of gazetteer features; sentence start and end position; Boolean-valued orthographic properties of the word form; string-valued surface properties of the word form; and morphological information.

We used the CoNLL standard method for evaluation. According to this, an automatic labeling is correct if it gives the same start and end position, and the same NE class as the gold standard. Based on this, precision and recall can be calculated, and the F-measure, as usual, the harmonic mean of these two values.

6.1 Wikipedia data

Our automatic annotation process retains all of the WP sentences which remained after our two-step filtering method, so sentences without NEs are also in-

	enwiki	enwiki filtered	CoNLL	huwiki	huwiki filtered	Szeged NER
token	60,520,819	21,718,854	302,811	19,108,027	3,512,249	225,963
NE	3,169,863	3,169,863	50,758	456,281	456,281	25,896
NE density	5.23%	14.59%	16.76%	2.38%	12.99%	11.46%

Table 2: Corpus size and NE density.

train	test	precision	recall	F-measure
CoNLL	CoNLL	85.13	85.13	85.13
enwiki	enwiki	72.46	73.33	72.89
enwiki	CoNLL	56.55	49.77	52.94
CoNLL with wikilists	CoNLL	86.33	86.35	86.34
CoNLL with wikitags	CoNLL	85.88	85.94	85.91

Table 3: English results.

cluded in the corpus. The rationale behind this is that we wanted to reserve the original distribution of names in WP as much as possible. However, after further investigation of the NE density in our corpora and gold standard corpora, we decided not to include the sentences without NEs in evaluation datasets.

Table 2 summarizes the data regarding corpus size and NE density. The English (enwiki) and the Hungarian WP (huwiki) corpora originally have the NE density of 5.23% and 2.38%, respectively. In comparison to the gold standard datasets (CoNLL, Szeged NER) these counts are quite low. It can be due to the difference between domains: newswire articles usually contain more NEs, typically ORG. The other reason might be that we discarded sentences containing unidentified NEs (cf. Section 3).

6.2 Experiments and results

The English WP corpus was evaluated against itself and a manually annotated English corpus. Since the filtered English WP corpus, containing only the sentences with NEs, is still very large, our experiments were performed with a sample of 3.5 million tokens, the size of our filtered Hungarian corpus, divided into train and test sets (90%-10%).

For English cross-corpus evaluation the CoNLL-2003 corpus was chosen. As is well known, training and testing across different corpora decreases F-measure. Domain differences certainly affect NER performance, and the different annotation schemes pose several compatibility problems. Nothman et al. (2008) showed that each set of gold standard training data performs better on corresponding test sets than on test sets from other sources. The situation here is similar (see Table 3 for results): the NE tagger trained on WP does not achieve as high performance tested against CoNLL test set (enwiki-CoNLL) as one trained on its own train set (enwiki-enwiki).

WP-derived corpora can also be used for improving NER accuracy in other ways. First, we collected gazetteer lists from the corpus for each NE category, which improved the overall F-measure given to the NE tagger training and testing on CoNLL dataset (CoNLL with wikilists). A second trial was labeling the CoNLL datasets by the model trained on WP corpus, and giving these labels as extra features to the next CoNLL train (CoNLL with wikitags). Both methods result in improved F-measure on CoNLL test set.

Since in Hungarian NE tagging we followed the Szeged NER corpus annotation guidelines, we performed the experiments on this dataset. Hungarian results are similar to the English ones (see Table 1), the only difference is that F-measures for Hungarian are significantly higher. This can be due to the fact that the MISC category for Hungarian contains less types of names, thus the inconsistency of this class is smaller (cf. Section 4). In contrast to the CoNLL corpus, the Szeged NER corpus was accurately annotated with an inter-annotator agreement over 99%.

Due to the quite good F-measure of training on

our Hungarian train corpus and testing on the corresponding test set, our Hungarian corpus can serve as a training corpus to build NE taggers for non-newswire domains.

7 Conclusion

We have presented freely available NE tagged corpora for English and Hungarian, fully automatically generated from WP. In contrast to the methods used so far for automatic annotation of NEs in WP texts, we applied a new approach, namely mapping DBpedia ontology classes to standard CoNLL NE tags, and assigning them to WP entities. Following Nothman (2008), the process can be divided into four main steps: classifying WP articles into entity classes; parsing WP and splitting articles into sentences; labeling NEs in the text; and selecting sentences for inclusion in the corpus.

The huge amount of WP articles opens the possibility of building large enough corpora for otherwise less resourced languages such as Hungarian. Due to the particularities of Hungarian, some steps are slightly different, and special linguistic phenomena pose several problems related to the NER task to solve.

Automatically generated corpora can be useful for improving NER in more ways. We showed that gazetteer lists extracted from our corpora, and training with extra features given by the model trained on our corpora, improve F-measure. Moreover, our Hungarian corpus can serve as a training corpus for more general domains than the classic newswire.

Acknowledgements

This research was supported by OTKA grant no. 82333 and the CESAR project under the ICT Policy Support Programme (grant no. 271022). The authors are grateful to Attila Zséder for his work on Wikipedia parsing and to András Kornai for his insightful comments.

References

Steven Bird, Ewan Klein, Edward Loper. 2009. *Natural Language Processing with Python.* O'Reilly Media Inc.

Christian Bizer, Jens Lehmann, Georgi Kobilarov, Sören Auer, Christian Becker, Richard Cyganiak, Sebastian Hellmann. 2009. DBpedia – A Crystallization Point for the Web of Data. In: *Journal of Web Semantics: Science, Services and Agents on the World Wide Web*, Issue 7, pages 154–165.

B. Bunescu and M. Pasca. 2006. Using encyclopedic knowledge for named entity disambiguation. In: *Proceedings of the 11th Conference of the European Chapter of the Association for Computational Linguistics*, pages 9–16.

Dóra Csendes, János Csirik, Tibor Gyimóthy. 2004. The Szeged Corpus: A POS tagged and Syntactically Annotated Hungarian Natural Language Corpus. In: *Proceedings of TSD 2004*, vol. 3206, pages 41–49.

S. Cucerzan. 2007. Large-scale named entity disambiguation based on Wikipedia data. In: *Proceedings of the 2007 Joint Conference on Empirical Methods in Natural Language Processing and Computational Natural Language Learning*. Prague, Czech Republic, June 2007. pages 708–716.

Ralph Grishman and B. Sundheim. 1996. Message Understanding Conference – 6. In: *Proc. International Conference on Computational Linguistics*.

P. Halácsy, A. Kornai and Cs. Oravecz. 2007. Hunpos – an open source trigram tagger. In: *Proceedings of the 45th Annual Meeting of the Association for Computational Linguistics*, pages 209–212.

Jun'ichi Kazama and Kentaro Torisawa. 2007. Exploiting Wikipedia as External Knowledge for Named Entity Recognition. In: *Proceedings of the 2007 Joint Conference on Empirical Methods in Natural Language Processing and Computational Natural Language Learning*, pages 698–707.

Tibor Kiss, Jan Strunk. 2006. Unsupervised Multilingual Sentence Boundary Detection. In: *Computational Linguistics*, 32 (4): pages 485–525.

András Kornai, Péter Rebrus, Péter Vajda, Péter Halácsy, András Rung, Viktor Trón. 2004. Általános célú morfológiai elemző kimeneti formalizmusa (The output formalism of a general-purpose morphological analyzer). In: *Proceedings of the 2nd Hungarian Computational Linguistics Conference.*

Olena Medelyan, David Milne, Catherine Legg, and Ian H. Witten. 2009. Mining meaning from Wikipedia. *International Journal of Human-Computer Studies*, 67: 716–754.

David Nadeau, Peter D. Turney and Stan Matwin. 2006. Unsupervised named entity recognition: Generating gazetteers and resolving ambiguity. In: *Proceedings of the 19th Canadian Conference on Artificial Intelligence*, volume 4013 of *LNCS*, pages 266–277.

Joel Nothman, James R. Curran, and Tara Murphy. 2008. Transforming Wikipedia into Named Entity Training Data. In: *Proceedings of the Australasian Language Technology Workshop*, Vol 6., pages 124–132.

Joel Nothman, Tara Murphy and James R. Curran. 2009. Analysing Wikipedia and Gold-Standard Corpora for NER Training. In: *Proceedings of the 12th Conference of the European Chapter of the ACL*, pages 612–620.

Alexander E. Richman and Patrick Schone. 2008. Mining Wiki Resources for Multilingual Named Entity Recognition. In: *Proceedings of ACL-08: HLT*, pages 1–9.

György Szarvas, Richárd Farkas, András Kocsor. 2006. A highly accurate Named Entity corpus for Hungarian. In: *Proceedings of International Conference on Language Resources and Evaluation.*

Erik F. Tjong Kim Sang. 2002. Introduction to the CoNLL-2002 shared task: Language-independent named entity recognition. In: *Proceedings of the 6th Conference on Natural Language Learning*, pages 1–4, Taipei, Taiwan.

Erik F. Tjong Kim Sang and Fien De Meulder. 2003. Introduction to the CoNLL-2003 shared task: Language-independent named entity recognition. In: *Proceedings of the 7th Conference on Natural Language Learning*, pages 142–147, Edmonton, Canada.

A. Toral and R. Muñoz. 2006. A proposal to automatically build and maintain gazetteers for Named Entity Recognition by using Wikipedia. In: *EACL 2006.*

Viktor Trón, György Gyepesi, Péter Halácsy, András Kornai, László Németh, Dániel Varga. 2005. Hunmorph: open source word analysis. In: *Proceedings of the ACL 2005 Workshop on Software.*

Dániel Varga and Eszter Simon. 2007. Hungarian named entity recognition with a maximum entropy approach. *Acta Cybernetica*, 18: 293–301.

H. Zaragoza and J. Atserias and M. Ciaramita and G. Attardi. 2007. Semantically Annotated Snapshot of the English Wikipedia v.1 (SW1). `http://www.yr-bcn.es/semanticWikipedia`

Rescoring a Phrase-based Machine Transliteration System with Recurrent Neural Network Language Models

Andrew Finch
NICT
3-5 Hikaridai
Keihanna Science City
619-0289 JAPAN
andrew.finch@nict.go.jp

Paul Dixon
NICT
3-5 Hikaridai
Keihanna Science City
619-0289 JAPAN
paul.dixon@nict.go.jp

Eiichiro Sumita
NICT
3-5 Hikaridai
Keihanna Science City
619-0289 JAPAN
eiichiro.sumita@nict.go.jp

Abstract

The system entered into this year's shared transliteration evaluation is implemented within a phrase-based statistical machine transliteration (SMT) framework. The system is based on a joint source-channel model in combination with a target language model and models to control the length of the sequences generated. The joint source-channel model was trained using a many-to-many Bayesian bilingual alignment. The focus of this year's system is on input representation. In order attempt to mitigate data sparseness issues in the joint source-channel model, we augmented the system with recurrent neural network (RNN) models that can learn to project the grapheme set onto a smaller hidden representation. We performed experiments on development data to evaluate the effectiveness of our approach. Our results show that using an RNN language model can improve performance for language pairs with large grapheme sets on the target side.

1 Introduction

Our system for the NEWS shared evaluation on transliteration generation is based on the system entered into last years evaluation (Finch et al., 2011). Some minor improvements have been made to some of the components, but the major difference is the addition of a re-scoring step with three rescoring models: an RNN target language model; an RNN joint source-channel model; and a maximum entropy model (this model was part of last year's system but has been moved from the decoding step into the re-scoring step for efficiency). In all our experiments we have taken a strictly language independent approach. Each of the language pairs were processed automatically from the graphemic representation supplied for the shared tasks, with no language specific treatment for any of the language pairs.

Recent research results on the application of recurrent neural network models to language modeling have shown that very promising reductions in text data perplexity relative to traditional n-gram language model approaches are possible (Mikolov et al., 2010; Mikolov et al., 2011). The RNN approach differs from the standard n-gram approach in that RNNs are able to smooth by projecting the grapheme set onto a set of hidden units, a process that effectively clusters similar graphemes. Furthermore, RNNs have been reported to be effective where data resources are limited (Kombrink et al., 2011).

These characteristics motivate us to investigate the effect of applying this approach in modeling at the grapheme (or grapheme sequence pair) level, particularly as two of the most important models in our system are both language models. The main drawback of RNN based models, their exceptionally high training computational complexity (Mikolov et al., 2010) is not an obstacle for training models for this shared task, though it may be an issue if large amounts of monolingual data are used to build the language models. We run experiments using this technique to investigate its effect on both corpus perplexity and end-to-end system performance (since it is not necessarily the case that gains in language model perplexity result in better systems (Chen et al., 1998)).

Throughout this paper we will refer to graphemes, grapheme sequences and grapheme sequence pairs. By grapheme, we mean a single unicode character, for example 'a' in English, 'ア' in Japanese or '明' in Chinese. Grapheme sequences are arbitrary sequences of these graphemes, and grapheme sequence pairs are 2-tuples of grapheme sequences, each element in the tuple being a grapheme sequence in a given language; for example: ('hello','ハロー').

2 System Description

2.1 Bilingual Bayesian Grapheme Alignment

To train the joint-source-channel model(s) in our system, we perform a many-to-many grapheme-to-grapheme alignment. To discover this alignment we use the Bayesian non-parametric technique described in (Finch and Sumita, 2010) which is a relative of the technique proposed by (Huang et al., 2011). Bayesian techniques typically build compact models with few parameters that do not overfit the data and have been shown to be effective for transliteration (Finch and Sumita, 2010; Finch et al., 2011).

2.2 Phrase-based SMT Models

The decoding was performed using a specially modified version of the OCTAVIAN decoder (Finch et al., 2007), an in-house multi-stack phrase-based decoder that operates on the same principles as the MOSES decoder (Koehn et al., 2007). This component of the system is implemented as a log-linear combination of 4 different models: a joint source-channel model; a target language model; a grapheme insertion penalty mode; and a grapheme sequence pair insertion penalty model. The following sections describe each of these models in detail. Due to the small size of many of the data sets in the shared tasks, we used all of the data to build models for the final systems.

2.2.1 N-gram joint source-channel model

The n-gram joint source-channel model used during decoding by the SMT decoder was trained from the Viterbi alignment arising from the final iteration of the Bayesian segmentation process on the training data (for the model used in parameter tuning), and the training data added to the development data (for the model used to decode the test data). We used the MIT language modeling toolkit (Bo-june et al., 2008) with modified Knesser-Ney smoothing to build this model. In all experiments we used a language model of order 5.

2.2.2 N-gram target Language model

The target model was trained from target side of the training data (for model used in parameter tuning), and the training data added to the development data (for the model used to decode the test data). We used the MIT language modeling toolkit with Knesser-Ney smoothing to build this model. In all experiments we used a language model of order 5.

2.2.3 Insertion penalty models

Both grapheme based and grapheme-sequence-pair-based insertion penalty models are simple models that add a constant value to their score each time a grapheme (or grapheme sequence pair) is added to the target hypotheses. These models control the tendency both of the joint source-channel model and the target language model to generate derivations that are too short.

2.3 Re-scoring Step

2.3.1 Overview

The system has a separate re-scoring stage that like the SMT models described in the previous section is implemented as a log-linear model. The log-linear weights are trained using the same MERT (Och, 2003) procedure. In principle, the weights for the models in this stage could be trained in a single step together with the SMT weights, and in last year's system this was the case for the ME model. However the models in this stage are more computationally expensive, and to reduce training time we train their weights in a second step. The three models used for re-scoring (20-best) are described in the following sections.

2.3.2 Maximum-entropy model

The maximum entropy model used for re-scoring embodies a set of features designed to take the local context of source and target graphemes and grapheme sequences into account. The features can be partitioned into two classes: grapheme-based features and grapheme sequence-based features. In both cases we use a context of 2 to the left and right for the source, and 2 to the left for the target. Sequence begin and end markers are added to both source and target and are used in the context. The features used in the ME model consist of all possible bigrams of contiguous elements in the context. We do not mix features at the grapheme level and grapheme sequence level, so for example, a grapheme sequence bigram can only consist of grapheme sequences (including sequences of length 1).

2.3.3 RNN Language models

We introduce two RNN language models (Mikolov et al., 2011) into the re-scoring step of our system. The first model is a language model over grapheme sequences in the target language; the second model is a joint source-channel model over bilingual grapheme sequence pairs. These models were trained on the same data as their

Language Pair	Accuracy in top-1	Mean F-score	MRR	MAP_{ref}
Arabic to English (ArEn)	0.588	0.930	0.709	0.507
Chinese to English (ChEn)	0.203	0.736	0.309	0.200
English to Bengali (Bangla) (EnBa)	0.460	0.891	0.583	0.458
English to Chinese (EnCh)	0.311	0.666	0.447	0.308
English to Hebrew (EnHe)	0.154	0.787	0.229	0.153
English to Hindi (EnHi)	0.668	0.923	0.738	0.661
English to Japanese Katakana (EnJa)	0.401	0.810	0.523	0.397
English to Kannada (EnKa)	0.546	0.901	0.641	0.545
English to Korean Hangul (EnKo)	0.384	0.721	0.465	0.383
English to Persian (EnPe)	0.655	0.941	0.774	0.643
English to Tamil (EnTa)	0.592	0.908	0.679	0.592
English to Thai (EnTh)	0.122	0.747	0.183	0.122
English to Japanese Kanji (JnJk)	0.513	0.693	0.598	0.419
Thai to English (ThEn)	0.140	0.766	0.216	0.140

Table 1: The evaluation results on the 2012 shared task for our system in terms of the official metrics.

n-gram counterparts described in Sections 2.2.1 and 2.2.2. The models were trained using the training procedure described in Section 3.1.

2.4 Parameter Tuning

The exponential log-linear model weights of both the SMT and re-scoring stages of our system were set by tuning the system on development data using the MERT procedure (Och, 2003) by means of the publicly available ZMERT toolkit [1] (Zaidan, 2009). The systems reported in this paper used a metric based on the word-level F-score, an official evaluation metric for the shared tasks (Zhang et al., 2012), which measures the relationship of the longest common subsequence of the transliteration pair to the lengths of both source and target sequences.

2.5 Official Results

The official scores for our system are given in Table 1. Some of the data tracks will benefit from a language-dependent treatment for example in Korean it is advantageous to decompose the characters, and other languages benefit from romanization as this can reduce data sparseness issue and allow the translation of unknown graphemes in test data.

3 Experiments

3.1 Perplexity

In this section we examine the performance of the RNN language model in terms of its perplexity on unseen data. For these experiments we divided the training into two parts: a training set (90% of the data) and a validation set (the remaining 10%), and used the development set as the test data on which the perplexity calculations were made.

The RNN model was built using the publicly available RNNLM toolkit [2]. A set of pilot experiments was run on subsets of the training data to find suitable values for the number of hidden units and number of classes used to train the RNN, and a simple grid search we used to find the best parameters for each language pair. All other parameters were left at their default values. The n-gram language model was trained using the SRI language modeling toolkit (Stolcke, 1999). We used a 5-gram model in these experiments trained with Witten-Bell smoothing.

Table 2 shows the results of this experiment. In 9 out of the 15 experiments the RNN language model had lower perplexity than the 5-gram backoff language model. Furthermore, in all of the experiments the interpolated model (a model formed by linearly interpolating the two models together with equal weights) had considerably lower perplexity than either component model. The largest relative gains were observed in Jn-Jk, En-Ko and En-Ch; these three languages had by far the largest grapheme set sizes out of all the language pairs. This result is not surprising because of the manner in which the RNN language models are able to smooth by projection of the grapheme set onto the set of hidden units.

[1] http://www.cs.jhu.edu/~ozaidan/zmert/

[2] http://www.fit.vutbr.cz/imikolov/rnnlm/index.html

Language Pair	RNN perplexity	N-gram perplexity	Interpolated perplexity	Grapheme set size	Corpus size (graphemes)	F-score with RNN	F-score no RNN
Ar-En	9.96	8.83	8.69	29	1683K	0.873	0.870
Ch-En	13.52	13.87	12.34	26	231K	0.896	0.882
En-Ba	12.30	11.00	10.73	59	78K	0.968	0.951
En-Ch	61.78	77.78	59.95	367	107K	0.883	0.866
En-He	9.78	10.27	9.51	34	49K	0.965	0.967
En-Hi	15.09	14.82	13.48	79	94K	0.980	0.977
En-Ja	19.52	20.16	18.51	81	132K	0.945	0.939
En-Ka	11.97	12.30	11.04	75	87K	0.967	0.969
En-Ko	45.06	50.41	44.79	700	19K	0.910	0.898
En-Pe	10.86	11.55	10.58	32	64K	0.933	0.937
En-Ta	9.23	9.49	8.60	63	93K	0.978	0.977
En-Th	8.40	8.23	7.67	64	207K	0.957	0.940
Jn-Jk	65.63	90.17	66.43	1536	44K	0.703	0.684
Th-En	10.20	9.37	8.98	43	166K	0.954	0.949

Table 2: Language model perplexity scores on the development set with n-gram, RNN and interpolated language models, together with system performance with and without the RNN models.

3.2 System Performance

In this section we look at whether the gains from incorporating the RNN language models result in gains in overall system performance. We ran experiments on the data used in the perplexity experiments. The only difference in the systems we compare was whether or not the RNN language models were included in the re-scoring process; the RNN model being effectively interpolated in a log-linear manner with the other models when it was included. MERT parameter tuning was performed separately for systems with and without the RNN models. The results in terms of F-score are shown in Table 2. The results show small gains in performance for 11 of the 14 language pairs, indicating that the RNN models are effective. Of the languages with larger grapheme set sizes that showed higher improvements in perplexity, two (Jn-Jk and En-Ch) showed larger than average improvement in overall system performance.

4 Conclusion

The system used for this year's shared evaluation was implemented within a phrase-based statistical machine translation framework augmented by a joint-source channel model trained from a many-to-many alignment of grapheme sequences using a Bayesian alignment approach. The system had a rescoring step that integrates features from a maximum entropy model with two RNN language models; one for the target grapheme sequence, and the other for the sequence of grapheme sequence pairs used to generate the target.

We ran experiments to determine the effectiveness of the RNN language models on the transliteration tasks. We found that the approach was generally effective and particularly effective for tasks with large grapheme set sizes.

In future work we would like to investigate alternative ways of integrating RNN models into our system. In particular it may be feasible to insert the models directly into the SMT component of our system so that they can be used directly in the decoding process. Furthermore, we intend to examine how the impact of these models in the case where larger corpora of monolingual data are used.

Acknowledgements

For the English-Japanese, English-Korean and Arabic-English datasets, the reader is referred to the CJK website: http://www.cjk.org. For English-Hindi, English-Tamil, and English-Kannada, and English-Bangla the data sets originated from the work of (Kumaran and Kellner, 2007) [3]. The Chinese language corpora came from the Xinhua news agency (Xinhua News Agency, 1992). The English Persian corpus originates from the work of (Karimi et al., 2006; Karimi et al., 2007).

[3] http://research.microsoft.com/india

References

Bo-june, Paul Hsu, and James Glass. 2008. Iterative language model estimation: Efficient data structure and algorithms. In *Proc. Interspeech*.

Stanley Chen, Douglas Beeferman, and Ronald Rosenfeld. 1998. Evaluation metrics for language models.

Andrew Finch and Eiichiro Sumita. 2010. A Bayesian Model of Bilingual Segmentation for Transliteration. In Marcello Federico, Ian Lane, Michael Paul, and François Yvon, editors, *Proceedings of the seventh International Workshop on Spoken Language Translation (IWSLT)*, pages 259–266.

Andrew Finch, Etienne Denoual, Hideo Okuma, Michael Paul, Hirofumi Yamamoto, Keiji Yasuda, Ruiqiang Zhang, and Eiichiro Sumita. 2007. The NICT/ATR speech translation system for IWSLT 2007. In *Proceedings of the IWSLT*, Trento, Italy.

Andrew Finch, Paul Dixon, and Eiichiro Sumita. 2011. Integrating models derived from non-parametric bayesian co-segmentation into a statistical machine transliteration system. In *Proceedings of the Named Entities Workshop*, pages 23–27, Chiang Mai, Thailand, Nov. Asian Federation of Natural Language Processing.

Yun Huang, Min Zhang, and Chew Lim Tan. 2011. Nonparametric Bayesian Machine Transliteration with Synchronous Adaptor Grammars. In *ACL (Short Papers)*, pages 534–539.

Sarvnaz Karimi, Andrew Turpin, and Falk Scholer. 2006. English to persian transliteration. In *SPIRE*, pages 255–266.

Sarvnaz Karimi, Andrew Turpin, and Falk Scholer. 2007. Corpus effects on the evaluation of automated transliteration systems. *Proceedings of the 45th Annual Meeting of the Association of Computational Linguistics*.

Philipp Koehn, Hieu Hoang, Alexandra Birch, Chris Callison-Burch, Marcello Federico, Nicola Bertoldi, Brooke Cowa, Wade Shen, Christine Moran, Richard Zens, Chris Dyer, Ondrej Bojar, Alexandra Constantin, and Evan Herbst. 2007. Moses: open source toolkit for statistical machine translation. In *ACL 2007: proceedings of demo and poster sessions*, pages 177–180, Prague, Czeck Republic, June.

Stefan Kombrink, Tomáš Mikolov, Martin Karafiát, and Lukáš Burget. 2011. Recurrent neural network based language modeling in meeting recognition. In *Proceedings of Interspeech 2011*, volume 2011, pages 2877–2880. International Speech Communication Association.

A. Kumaran and Tobias Kellner. 2007. A generic framework for machine transliteration. In *SIGIR'07*, pages 721–722.

Tomáš Mikolov, Martin Karafiát, Lukáš Burget, Jan Černocký, and Sanjeev Khudanpur. 2010. Recurrent neural network based language model. In *Proceedings of the 11th Annual Conference of the International Speech Communication Association (INTERSPEECH 2010)*, volume 2010, pages 1045–1048. International Speech Communication Association.

Tomáš Mikolov, Anoop Deoras, Stefan Kombrink, Lukáš Burget, and Jan Černocký. 2011. Empirical evaluation and combination of advanced language modeling techniques. In *Proceedings of Interspeech 2011*, volume 2011, pages 605–608. International Speech Communication Association.

Franz J. Och. 2003. Minimum error rate training for statistical machine translation. In *Proceedings of the ACL*.

Andreas Stolcke. 1999. Srilm - an extensible language model toolkit.

Xinhua News Agency. 1992. Chinese transliteration of foreign personal names. *The Commercial Press*.

Omar F. Zaidan. 2009. Z-MERT: A fully configurable open source tool for minimum error rate training of machine translation systems. *The Prague Bulletin of Mathematical Linguistics*, 91:79–88.

Min Zhang, Haizhou Li, Liu Ming, and A. Kumaran. 2012. Whitepaper of news 2012 shared task on machine transliteration. In *Proceedings of the 2012 Named Entities Workshop*, Jeju, Korea. Association for Computational Linguistics.

Syllable-based Machine Transliteration with Extra Phrase Features

Chunyue Zhang, Tingting Li, Tiejun Zhao
MOE-MS Key Laboratory of Natural Language Processing and Speech
Harbin Institute of Technology
Harbin,China
{cyzhang,ttli,tjzhao}@mtlab.hit.edu.cn

Abstract

This paper describes our syllable-based phrase transliteration system for the NEWS 2012 shared task on English-Chinese track and its back. Grapheme-based Transliteration maps the character(s) in the source side to the target character(s) directly. However, character-based segmentation on English side will cause ambiguity in alignment step. In this paper we utilize Phrase-based model to solve machine transliteration with the mapping between Chinese characters and English syllables rather than English characters. Two heuristic rule-based syllable segmentation algorithms are applied. This transliteration model also incorporates three phonetic features to enhance discriminative ability for phrase. The primary system achieved 0.330 on Chinese-English and 0.177 on English-Chinese in terms of top-1 accuracy.

1 Introduction

Machine transliteration, based on the pronunciation, transforms the script of a word from a source language to a target language automatically.

With a continuous growth of out-of-vocabulary names to be transliterated, the traditional dictionary-based methods are no longer suitable. So data-driven method is gradually prevailing now, and many new approaches are explored.

Knight(1998) proposes a phoneme-based approach to solve the transliteration between English names and Japanese katakana. It makes use of a common phonetic representation as a pivot. The phoneme-based approach needs a pronunciation dictionary for one or two languages. These dictionaries usually do not exist or can't cover all the names. So grapheme-based(Li et al., 2004) approach has gained lots of attention recently. Huang(2011) proposes a novel nonparametric Bayesian using synchronous adaptor grammars to model the grapheme-based transliteration. Zhang(2010) builds the pivot transliteration model with grapheme-based method.

The hybrid approach tries to utilize both phoneme and grapheme information, and usually integrates the output of multiple engines to improve transliteration. Oh and Choi(2006) integrate both phoneme and grapheme features into a single leaning framework.

As an instance of grapheme-based approach, Jia(2009) views machine transliteration as a special example of machine translation and uses the phrase-based machine translation model to solve it. The approach is simple and effective. Our paper follows this way. However, using the English letters and Chinese characters as basic mapping units will make ambiguity in the alignment and translation step. One Chinese character usually maps one syllable, so syllabifying English words can be more discriminative.

We present a solution to this ambiguity by replacing the English character with an English syllable which is consecutive characters and can keep some phonetic properties. For this purpose, two heuristic and simple syllable segmentation algorithms are used to syllabify English side into syllables sequence. Besides two above, three extra phrase features for transliteration are used to enhance the model.

The rest of this paper is organized as follows. Section 2 introduces the phrase-based model briefly. Section 3 describes two rule-based syllable segmentation methods and three new special features for transliteration in detail. Experiments and analyses are discussed in section 4. Conclusions and future work are addressed in section 5.

2 Phrase-based Machine Transliteration Model

Machine transliteration can be regarded as a special instance of machine translation. Jia(2009) solves transliteration with phrase-based model firstly. There an English character is treated as a word in machine translation. On the contrast, character is replaced by syllable in this paper. Then transliteration can be viewed as a pure translation task. The phrase-based machine transliteration can be formulated by equation 1.

$$\tilde{e} = \arg\max_{e} p(x) = \exp \sum_{i=1}^{n} \lambda_i h_i(x) \quad (1)$$

- n is the number of features
- λ_i is the weight of feature i

In our phrase-based transliteration system, the following features are used by default:

- the bidirectional probability between source phrase and the target phrase
- The bidirectional lexical probability between source phrase and target phrase
- the fluency of the output, namely language model
- the length penalty

3 Syllable Segmentation and Extra Phrase Features

This section describes two rule-based syllable segmentation algorithms and three extra phrase features added to machine transliteration model.

3.1 Syllable Segmentation Algorithm

In (Jia et al., 2009), the basic alignment units are English character and Chinese character(called c2c). This setup is the simplest format to implement the model. However, transliteration from English to Chinese usually maps an English syllable to a single Chinese character. As one Chinese character usually corresponds to many English characters, the c2c method has only a modest discriminative ability. Obviously syllabifying English is more suitable for this situation. Yang(2010) utilizes a CRF-based segmentor to syllabify English and Kwong(2011) syllabifies English with the Onset First Principle. Alternatively, inspired by (Jiang, 2007), two heuristic rule-based methods are addressed to syllabify the English names in this paper.

Given an English name *E*, it can be syllabified into a syllable sequence *SE* = {*e1,e2,...,en*} with one of the following two linguistic methods.

Simple Segmentation Algorithm(SSA):

1. {'*a*', '*o*' , '*e*', '*i*', '*u*'} are defined as vowels. '*y*' is defined as a vowel when it is not followed by a vowel; '*r*' is defined as a vowel when it follows a vowel and is followed by a consonant[1]. All other characters are defined as consonants; this forms the basic vowel set;
2. A consecutive vowels sequence, formed by the basic vowel set, is treated as a new vowel symbol; Step 1 and 2 form the new vowel set;
3. A consonant and its following vowel are treated as a syllable;
4. Consecutive consonants are separated; a vowel symbol(in the new vowel set) followed by a consonant is separated;
5. The rest isolated characters sequences are regarded as individual syllables in each word.

SSA treats all the consecutive vowels as a single new vowel simply. In fact, many consecutive vowels like "*io*" often align two or more Chinese characters, such as " *zio* 西 奥". It is better to separate it as two syllables rather than one syllable in alignment step. So we present another segment algorithm which takes more details into consideration.

Fine-grained Segment Algorithm(FSA):

1. Replace '*x*' in English names with '*k s*' firstly;
2. {'*a*','*o*','*e*','*i*','*u*'} are defined as vowels. '*y*' is defined as a vowel when it is not followed by a vowel;
3. When '*w*' follows '*a*','*e*','*o*' and isn't followed by '*h*', treat '*w*' and the preceding vowel as a new vowel symbol; Step 2 and 3 form the basic vowel set;
4. A consecutive vowels sequence which is formed by the basic vowel set is treated as a new vowel

[1] A review points the SSA lacking of ability to deal with '*h*'. We leave it for the future work.

symbol, excepting *'iu'*, *'eo'*, *'io'*, *'oi'*, *'ia'*, *'ui'*, *'ua'*, *'uo'* ; Step 2, 3 and 4 form the new vowel set;
5. Consecutive consonants are separated; a vowel symbol(in the new vowel set) followed by a consonant sequence is separated;
6. A consonant and its following vowel are treated as a syllable; the rest of the isolated consonants and vowels are regarded as individual syllables in each word.

After segmenting the English characters sequence, the new transliteration units, syllables, will be more discriminative.

3.2 Extra phrase features

The default features of phrase can't express the special characteristic of transliteration. We propose three features trying to explore the transliteration property.

Begin and End Feature(BE)

When a Chinese character is chosen as the corresponding transliteration, its position in the transliteration result is important. Such as a syllable "*zu*" that can be transliterate into "朱" or "祖" in Chinese while "朱" will be preferred if it appears at the beginning position.

To explore this kind of information, the pseudo characters "B" and "E" are added to the train and test data. So in the extracted phrase table, "B" always precedes the Chinese character that prefers at the first position, and "E" always follows the Chinese character that appears at the last position.

Phrase Length Feature

Chinese character can be pronounced according to its pinyin format which is written like English word. And the longer English syllable is, the longer pinyin format it often has. So the length information of Chinese character and its pinyin can be used to disambiguate the phrase itself. Here we definite two new features to address it. Suppose <e,c> as a phrase pair, e= {e1,e2,...,em},c = {c1,c2,...,cn},ei stands for an English syllable and ci stands for a Chinese character. p(ci) is the pinyin format of ci. #(ei) is equal to the number of characters in a syllable. #p(cj) is equal to the number of characters in a pinyin sequence. And then,

$$L1 = Sum(\#(ei)) / Sum(\#(p(cj))$$
$$L2 = m / n$$

4 Experiments

This section describes the data sets, experimental setup, experimental results and analyses.

4.1 Data Sets

The training set of English-Chinese transliteration track contains 37753 pairs of names. We pick up 3000 pairs from the training data randomly as the closed test set and the rest 34753 pairs as our training data set. In the official dev set some semantic translation pairs are found, such as "REPUBLIC OF CUBA 古巴共和国", and some many-to-one cases like "SHELL BEACH 谢尔比奇" also appear. We modify or delete these cases from the original dev set. At last, 3223 pairs are treated as the final dev set to tune the weights of system features.

Language	Segmentation Algorithm	Number
English	Character-based	6.82
	SSA	4.24
	FSA	4.48
Chinese	Character-based	3.17

Table 1: Average syllables of names based on different segmentation methods

Language	Segmentation Algorithm	Number
English	Character-based	26
	SSA	922
	FSA	463
Chinese	Character-based	368

Table 2 :Total number of unique units

For the Chinese-English back transliteration track, the final training and test sets are formed in the same way; the original dev set is used directly.

Here we use Character-based which treats single character as a "syllable", Simple and Fine-grained segmentation algorithms to deal with English names. Table 1 and table 2 show some syllabic statistics information. Table 1 shows the average syllables of the three segmentation approaches in training data. Table 2 shows the total number of unique units.

4.2 Experimental Setup

The Moses (Koehn et al., 2007) is used to implement the model in this paper. The Srilm(Stolcke et al., 2002) toolkit is used to count n-gram on the target of the training set. Here we use a 3-gram language model. In the transliteration model training step, the Giza++(Och et al., 2003) generates the alignment with the grow-diag-and-final heuristic, while other setup is default. In order to guarantee monotone decoding, the distortion distance is limited to 0. The MERT is used to tune model's weights. The method of (Jia et al., 2009) is the baseline setup.

4.3 Evaluation Metrics

The following 4 metrics are used to measure the quality of the transliteration results (Li et al., 2009a): Word Accuracy in Top-1 (ACC), Fuzziness in Top-1 (Mean F-score), Mean Reciprocal Rank (MRR), MAPref.

4.4 Results

Table 3 shows the performance of our system corresponding to baseline, SSA and FSA on the closed test set of EnCh track. BE, L1,L2 and BE+L1+L2 are implemented on the basis of FSA.

	ACC	Mean F-score	MRR	MAPref
Baseline	0.628	0.847	0.731	0.628
SSA	0.639	0.850	0.738	0.639
FSA	0.661	0.861	0.756	0.661
BE	0.648	0.856	0.751	0.648
L1	0.661	0.864	0.756	0.661
L2	0.619	0.844	0.727	0.619
BE+L1+L2	0.665	0.863	0.762	0.665

Table 3:The held-in results of EnCh

Table 3 shows that the forward transliteration performance gets consistent improvement from baseline to FSA. None of new three features can improve by self, while combining three features can gain a little.

	ACC	Mean F-score	MRR	MAPref
EnCh_Pri	0.330	0.676	0.408	0.319
EnCh_2	0.317	0.667	0.399	0.308
ChEn_pri	0.177	0.702	0.257	0.173

Table 4: The final official results of EnCh and ChEn

According to the performance of closed test, the transliteration results of EnCh and ChEn based on BE+L1+L2 are chosen as the primary submissions(EnCh_Pri and ChEn_Pri). And the result of FSA is the contrastive submission(EnCh_2). The table 4 shows the final official results of EnCh and ChEn.

5 Conclusions and future work

This paper uses the phrase-based machine translation to model the transliteration task and the state-of-the-art translation system Moses is used to implement it. We participate in the NEWS 2012 Machine Transliteration Shared Task English-Chinese and Chinese-English tracks.

To improve the capability of the basic phrase-based machine transliteration, two heuristic and rule-based English syllable segmentation methods are addressed. System can also be more robust with combination of three new special features for transliteration. The experimental results show that the Fine-grained Segmentation can improve the performance remarkably in English-Chinese transliteration track.

In the future, extensive error analyses will be made and methods will be proposed according to the specific error type. More syllable segmentation methods such as statistical-based will be tried.

Acknowledgments

The authors would like to thank all the reviews for their help about correcting grammatical errors of this paper and invaluable suggestions. This work is supported by the project of National High Technology Research and Development Program of China (863 Program) (No. 2011AA01A207) and the project of National Natural Science Foundation of China (No. 61100093).

References

Andreas Stolcke. 2002. SRILM - an Extensible Language Modeling Toolkit. In Proc. of ICSLP, Denver, USA.

Dong Yang, Paul Dixon and Sadaoki Furui. 2010. Jointly optimizing a two-step conditional random field model for machine transliteration and its fast decoding algorithm. In Proceedings of the ACL 2010 Conference Short Papers. pp. 275--280 Uppsala, Sweden.

Franz Josef Och, Hermann Ney. 2003. A systematic comparison of various statistical alignment models. Comput.Linguistics 29, 1, 19–51.

Haizhou Li , Min Zhang, Jian Su. 2004. A Joint Source Channel Model for Machine Transliteration. In Proceedings of the 42nd ACL, pp. 159-166.

Kevin Knight, Jonathan Graehl. 1998. Machine Transliteration. Computational Linguistics, Vol. 24, No. 4, pp. 599-612.

Long Jiang , Ming Zhou , Leefeng Chien and Cheng Niu. Named entity translation with web mining and transliteration, Proceedings of the 20th international joint conference on Artifical intelligence, p.1629-1634, January 06-12, 2007, Hyderabad, India

Min Zhang, Xiangyu Duan, Vladimir Pervouchine, and Haizhou Li. 2010. Machine transliteration: Leveraging on third languages. In Coling 2010: Posters, pages 1444–1452, Beijing, China, August. Coling 2010 Organizing Committee.

Oi Yee Kwong. 2011. English-Chinese Personal Name Transliteration by Syllable-Based Maximum Matching. In the Proceedings of the 2011 Named Entities Workshop,2011,pp.96-100.

Philipp Koehn, Hieu Hoang, Marcello Federico Nicola Bertoldi , Brooke Cowan and Wade Shen . 2007. Moses: Open Source Toolkit for Statistical Machine Translation. In Proceedings of the 45th ACL Companion Volume of the Demo and Poster Sessions, pp. 177-180.

Yun Huang, Min Zhang and Chewlim Tan. 2011. Nonparametric Bayesian Machine Transliteration with Synchronous Adaptor Grammars. In Proceedings of ACL-HLT 2011: Short Papers,Portland, Oregon, pp.534-539.

Yuxiang Jia, Danqing Zhu, and Shiwen Y. 2009. A Noisy Channel Model for Grapheme-based Machine Transliteration, In the Proceedings of the 2009 Named Entities Workshop, 2009, pp. 88-91.

English-Korean Named Entity Transliteration Using Substring Alignment and Re-ranking Methods

Chun-Kai Wu[†] **Yu-Chun Wang**[‡] **Richard Tzong-Han Tsai**[†]
[†]Department of Computer Science and Engineering,
Yuan Ze University, Taiwan
[‡]Department of Computer Science and Information Engineering,
National Taiwan University, Taiwan
s983301@mail.yzu.edu.tw d97023@csie.ntu.edu.tw
thtsai@saturn.yzu.edu.tw

Abstract

In this paper, we describe our approach to English-to-Korean transliteration task in NEWS 2012. Our system mainly consists of two components: an letter-to-phoneme alignment with m2m-aligner,and transliteration training model DirecTL-p. We construct different parameter settings to train several transliteration models. Then, we use two re-ranking methods to select the best transliteration among the prediction results from the different models. One re-ranking method is based on the co-occurrence of the transliteration pair in the web corpora. The other one is the JLIS-Reranking method which is based on the features from the alignment results. Our standard and non-standard runs achieves 0.398 and 0.458 in top-1 accuracy in the generation task.

1 Introduction

Named entity translation is a key problem in many NLP research fields such as machine translation, cross-language information retrieval, and question answering. Most name entity translation is based on transliteration, which is a method to map phonemes or graphemes from source language into target language. Therefore, named entity transliteration system is important for translation.

In the shared task, we focus on English-Korean transliteration. We consider to transform the transliteration task into a sequential labeling problem. We adopt m2m-aligner and DirecTL-p (Jiampojamarn et al., 2010) to do substring mapping and transliteration predicting, respectively. With this approach (Jiampojamarn et al., 2010) achieved promising results on NEWS 2010 transliteration tasks. In order to improve the transliteration performance, we also apply several ranking techniques to select the best Korean transliteration.

This paper is organized as following. In section 2 we describe the main approach we use including how we deal with the data, the alignment and training methods and our re-ranking techniques. In section 3, we show and discuss our results on English-Korean transliteration task. And finally the conclusion is in section 4.

2 Our Approach

In this section, we describe our approach for English-Korean transliteration which comprises the following steps:

1. Pre-processing
2. Letter-to-phoneme alignment
3. DirecTL-p training
4. Re-ranking results

2.1 Pre-processing

Korean writing system, namely *Hangul*, is alphabetical. However, unlike western writing system with Latin alphabets, Korean alphabet is composed into syllabic blocks. Each Korean syllabic block represent a syllable which has three components: initial consonant, medial vowel and optionally final consonant. Korean has 14 initial consonants, 10 medial vowels, and 7 final consonants. For instance, the syllabic block "신" (sin) is composed with three letters:

a initial consonant "ㅅ" (s), a medial vowel "ㅣ" (i), and a final consonant "ㄴ" (n).

For transliteration from English to Korean , we have to break each Korean syllabic blocks into two or three Korean letters. Then, we convert these Korean letters into Roman letters according to Revised Romanization of Korean for convenient processing.

2.2 Letter-to-phoneme Alignment

After obtaining English and Romanized Korean name entity pair, we generate the alignment between each pair by using m2m-aligner.

Since English orthography might not reflect its actual phonological forms, it makes one-to-one character alignment between English and Korean not practical.

Compared with traditional one-to-one alignment, the m2m-aligner overcomes two problems: One is double letters where two letters are mapped to one phoneme. English may use several characters for one phoneme which is presented in one letter in Korean, such as "ch" to "ㅊ" and "oo" to "ㅜ". However, one-to-one alignment only allows one letter to be mapped to one phoneme, so it must have to add an null phoneme to achieve one-to-one alignment. It may interfere with the transliteration prediction model.

The other problem is double phonemes problem where one letter is mapped to two phonemes. For example, the letter "x" in the English name entity "Texas" corresponds to two letters "ㄱ" and "ㅅ" in Korean. Besides, some English letters in the word might not be pronounced, like "k" in the English word "knight". We can eliminate this by pre-processing the data to find out double phonemes and merge them into single phoneme. Or we can add an null letter to it, but this may also disturb the prediction model. While performing alignments, m2m aligner allows us to set up the maximum length substring in source language (with the parameter x) and in target language (with the parameter y). Thus, when aligning, we set both parameter x and y to two because we think there are at most 2 English letters mapped to 2 Korean letters. To capture more double phonemes, we also have another parameter set with $x = 1$ and $y = 2$.

As mentioned in previous section, Korean syllabic block is composed of three or two letters. In order to cover more possible alignments, we construct another alignment configurations to take null consonant into consideration. Consequently, for any Korean syllabic block containing two Korean letters will be converted into three Roman letters with the third one being a predefined Roman letter representing null consonant. We also have two set of parameters for this change, that is $x = 2$, $y = 3$ and $x = 1$,$y = 3$. The reason we increase both y by one is that there are three Korean letters for each word.

2.3 DirecTL-p Training

With aligned English-Korean pairs, we can train our transliteration model. We apply DirecTL-p (Jiampojamarn et al., 2008) for our training and testing task. We train the transliteration models with different alignment parameter settings individually mentioned in section 2.2.

2.4 Re-ranking Results

Because we train several transliteration models with different alignment parameters, we have to combine the results from different models. Therefore, the re-ranking method is necessary to select the best transliteration result. For re-ranking, we propose two approaches.

1. Web-based re-ranking
2. JLIS-Reranking

2.4.1 Web-based re-ranking

The first re-ranking method is based on the occurrence of transliterations in the web corpora. We send each English-Korean transliteration pair generated by our transliteration models to Google web search engine to get the co-occurrence count of the pair in the retrieval results. But the result number may vary a lot, most of them will get millions of results while some will only get a few hundred.

2.4.2 JLIS-Reranking

In addition to web-based re-ranking approach, we also adopt JLIS-Reranking (Chang et al., 2010) to re-rank our results for the standard run. For an English-Korean transliteration pair, we can measure if they are actual transliteration of each other by observing the alignment between them. Since

Table 1: Results on development data.

Run	Accuracy	Mean F-score	MRR	MAP_{ref}
1 ($x = 2$, $y = 2$)	0.488	0.727	0.488	0.488
2 ($x = 1$, $y = 2$)	0.494	0.730	0.494	0.494
3 ($x = 1$, $y = 3$, with *null* consonant)	0.452	0.713	0.452	0.452
4 ($x = 2$, $y = 3$, with *null* consonant)	0.474	0.720	0.474	0.473
Web-based Reranking	0.536	0.754	0.563	0.536
JLIS-Reranking	0.500	0.737	0.500	0.500

Table 2: Results on test data

Run	Accuracy	Mean F-score	MRR	MAP_{ref}
Standard (JLIS-Reranking)	0.398	0.731	0.398	0.397
Non-standard (Web-based reranking)	0.458	0.757	0.484	0.458

DirecTL-p model outputs a file containing the alignment of each result, there are some features in the results that we can use for re-ranking. In our re-ranking approach, there are three features used in the process: *source grapheme chain* feature, *target grapheme chain* feature and *syllable consistent* feature. These three feature are proposed in (Song et al., 2010).

Source grapheme chain feature: This feature can tell us that how the source characters are aligned. Take "A|D|A|M" for example, we will get three chains which are A|D, D|A and A|M. With this feature we may know the alignment in the source language.

Target grapheme chain feature: Similar to the above feature, it tell us how the target characters are aligned. Take "NG:A:n|D|A|M" for example, which is the Korean transliteration of ADAM, we will get three chains which are n|D, D|A and A|M. With this feature we may know the alignment in the target language. "n" is the predefined null consonant.

Syllable consistent feature: We use this feature to measure syllable counts in both English and Korean. For English, we apply an Perl module[1] to measure the syllable counts. And for Korean, we simply count the number of syllabic blocks. This feature may guard our results, since a wrong prediction may not have the same number of syllable.

[1]http://search.cpan.org/~gregfast/Lingua-EN-Syllable-0.251/Syllable.pm

Other than the feature vectors created by above features, there is one important field when training the re-ranker, performance measure. For this field, we give it 1 when we predict a correct result otherwise we give it 0 since we think it is useless to get a partially correct result.

3 Result

To measure the transliteration models with different alignment parameters and the re-ranking methods, we construct several runs for experiments as follows.

- Run 1: m2m-aligner with parameters $x = 2$ and $y = 2$.
- Run 2: m2m-aligner with parameters $x = 1$ and $y = 2$.
- Run 3: m2m-aligner with parameters $x = 1$ and $y = 3$ and add null consonants in the Korean romanized representation.
- Run 4: m2m-aligner with parameters $x = 2$ and $y = 3$ and add null consonants in the Korean romanized representation.
- Web-based reranking: re-rank the results from run 1 to 4 based on Google search results.
- JLIS-Reranking: re-rank the results from run 1 to 4 based on JLIS-rerakning features.

Table 1 shows our results on the development data. As we can see in this table, Run 2 is better than Run 1 by 6 NEs. It may be that the data in develop set are double phonemes. And we also observe that both Run 1 and Run 2 is better than Run 3 and Run 4, the reason may be that the extra null consonant distract the performance of the prediction model.

From the results, it shows that our re-ranking methods can actually improve transliteration. Reranking based on web corpora can achieve better accuracy compared with web-based reranking. The JLIS-Reranking method slightly improve the accuracy. It could be that the features we use are not enough to capture the alignment between English-Korean NE pair.

Because the runs with re-ranking achieving better results, we submit the result on the test data with JLIS-Reranking as the standard run, and the result with the web-based re-ranking as the non-standard run for our final results. The results on the test data set are shown in table 2. The results also shows that the web-based re-ranking can achieve the best accuracy up to 0.458.

4 Conclusion

In this paper, we describe our approach to English-Korean named entity transliteration task for NEWS 2012. First, we decompose Korean word into Korean letters and then romanize them into sequential Roman letters. Since a Korean word may not contain the final consonant, we also create some alignment results with the null consonant in romanized Korean representations. After preprocessing the training data, we use m2m-aligner to get the alignments from English to Korean. Next, we train several transliteration models based on DirecTL-p with the alignments from the m2m-aligner. Finally, we propose two re-ranking methods. One is web-based re-ranking with Google search engine. We send the English NE and its Korean transliteration pair our model generates to Google to get the co-occurrence count to re-rank the results. The other method is JLIS-reranking based on three features from the alignment results, including source grapheme chain feature, target grapheme chain feature, and syllable consistent feature. In the experiment results, our method achieves the good accuracy up to 0.398 in the standard run and 0.458 in non-standard run. Our results show that the transliteration model with a web-based re-ranking method can achieve better accuracy in English-Korean transliteration.

References

Ming-Wei Chang, Vivek Srikumar, Dan Goldwas-ser, and Dan Roth. 2010. Structured output learning with indirect supervision. *Proceeding of the International Conference on Machine Learning (ICML).*

Sittichai Jiampojamarn, Grzegorz Kondrak, and Tarek Sherif. 2007. Applying many-to-many alignments and hidden markov models to letter-to-phoneme conversion. *Association for Computational Linguistics*, pages 372–379.

Sittichai Jiampojamarn, Colin Cherry, and Grzegorz Kondrak. 2008. Joint processing and discriminative training for letter-to-phoneme conversion. *Association for Computational Linguistics*, pages 905–912.

Sittichai Jiampojamarn, Kenneth Dwyer, Shane Bergsma, Aditya Bhargava, Qing Dou, Mi-Young Kim, and Grzegorz Kondrak. 2010. Transliteration generation and mining with limited training resources. *Proceedings of the 2010 Named Entities Workshop, ACL 2010*, pages 39–47.

Yan Song, Chunyu Kit, and Hai Zhao. 2010. Reranking with multiple features for better transliteration. *Proceedings of the 2010 Named Entities Work-shop, ACL 2010*, pages 62–65.

Applying mpaligner to Machine Transliteration with Japanese-Specific Heuristics

Yoh Okuno
Job Hunter
nokuno@nokuno.jp

Abstract

We developed a machine transliteration system combining mpaligner (an improvement of m2m-aligner), DirecTL+, and some Japanese-specific heuristics for the purpose of NEWS 2012. Our results show that mpaligner is greatly better than m2m-aligner, and the Japanese-specific heuristics are effective for JnJk and EnJa tasks. While m2m-aligner is not good at long alignment, mpaligner performs well at longer alignment without any length limit. In JnJk and EnJa tasks, it is crucial to handle long alignment. An experimental result revealed that de-romanization, which is reverse operation of romanization, is crucial for JnJk task. In EnJa task, it is shown that mora is the best alignment unit for Japanese language.

1 Introduction

NEWS 2012 shared task regards transliteration as phonetic translation of proper nouns across different languages (Zhang et al., 2012). The most common approach for automatic transliteration is to follow the manner of statistical machine translation (Finch and Sumita, 2008). This approach mainly consists of 3 steps below.

1. Align training data monotonically
2. Train discriminative model given aligned data
3. Decode input characters to n-best candidate

One of the most popular alignment tools is m2m-aligner (Jiampojamarn et al., 2007), which is released as an open source software [1]. DirecTL+ (Jiampojamarn et al., 2008) is a decoding and training tool [2] and can be used with m2m-aligner for transliteration generation task.

However, m2m-aligner is not good at long alignment with no length limit. It tends to overfit for long alignment since its training is based on maximum likelihood estimation. Finch and Sumita (2010) proposed non-parametric Bayesian co-segmentation and applied it to machine transliteration (Finch et al., 2011). They penalized long alignment adopting Poisson distribution as prior of word length in the Bayesian model. Another method to penalize long alignment is proposed by Kubo et al. (2011) and released as mpaligner [3], originally developed for the purpose of Japanese pronunciation prediction. Just for its availability, we used mpaligner as an alternative of m2m-aligner.

Since m2m-aligner and mpaligner are both character-based alignment, there is a problem to produce phonetically invalid alignment. That is, character-based alignment may divide atomic units of characters, called mora, into meaningless pieces. Ideally, mora-to-mora alignment should be used for this task while no training data is provided for such purpose. In this paper, we propose Japanese-specific heuristics to cope with this problem depending on language-specific knowledge.

[1] http://code.google.com/p/m2m-aligner/
[2] http://code.google.com/p/directl-p/
[3] http://sourceforge.jp/projects/mpaligner/

2 Related Works

Beside general researches for machine transliteration, there are other researches related to Japanese language. Cherry and Suzuki (2009) applied discriminative training to English-name-to-Japanese-Katakana transliteration. Hatori and Suzuki (2011) proposed a statistical machine translation approach for Japanese pronunciation prediction task. Hagiwara and Sekine (2011) used latent class model for transliteration including English-to-Japanese.

3 mpaligner: Minimum Pattern Aligner

mpaligner (Kubo et al., 2011) is an improvement of m2m-aligner. Their idea is simple; to penalize long alignment by scaling its probability using sum of their length. More formally, mpaligner uses a model;

$$P(x, y) = p_{x,y}{}^{|x|+|y|} \qquad (1)$$

when deletion and insertion are not allowed. Here, x and y are source and target strings, $P(x, y)$ is probability of string pair (x, y), $p_{x,y}$ is a parameter which is estimated by previous iteration, and $|x|+|y|$ is sum of length of strings x and y. Though the scaled probability is no longer normalized, M-step of EM algorithm performs a kind of normalization.

4 Japanese-Specific Heuristics

Since mpaligner is a general-purpose alignment tool, we developed Japanese-specific heuristics as preprocessing for training data. That is, our system regards combined characters as one character, and applies mpaligner to them.

4.1 Romanized Japanese Name to Japanese Kanji Back-Transliteration Task (JnJk)

The most important heuristic for JnJk task is *deromanization*, which is the reverse operation of romanization. In Japanese language, consonants and vowels are coupled and expressed as Kana characters. Since Kana characters should not be divided, de-romanization converts romanized Japanese to Kana characters. This enables the system to align Kana character as minimal unit. For this conversion, a common romanization table for Japanese input method is used [4]. Moreover, a silent character called *Sokuon* is combined with its previous character since it can not be aligned alone.

Table 1 shows basic conversion table. We adopt longest-match algorithm to replace sequence of Roman characters to Kana characters. Without these operations, characters like "KA" may wrongly divided into "K" and "A" and aligned to different Kanji characters. More detailed examples are described in table 2. The bold rows are correct alignemnts performed by deromanization.

4.2 English to Japanese Katakana Task (EnJa)

In EnJa task, the alignment unit of target side should be mora, not character. For this purpose, our system combines lower case characters with their previous characters. Moreover, Japanese hyphen is also combined with the previous one since they form one mora.

As a result, "ァ", "ィ", "ゥ", "ェ", "ォ", "ヶ", "ヵ", "ャ", "ュ", "ョ", "ッ", "ー" are combined with their previous characters and treated as one mora. Table 3 shows alignment examples with and without this heuristics.

5 Experiments

In this section, we show the official scores for 8 language pairs and further investigation for JnJk and EnJa tasks.

5.1 Official Scores for 8 Language Pairs

Table 4 shows the official scores for 8 language pairs. In the official submits, we used mpaligner for alignment and DirecTL+ for training and decoding. We tried two version of mpaligner, 0.9 and 0.97, and chose better one as the primary submission. The version of DirecTL+ is 1.1, and the iteration number is selected automatically by the development set. For JnJk and EnJa tasks, we used our heuristics described above. For other language pairs, we just applied mpaligner and DirecTL+ using their default settings.

The results seem good, and we can find that ChEn, EnCh, EnHe and JnJk are difficult tasks in both measures ACC and F-Score.

[4] http://www.social-ime.com/romaji-table.html

Table 1: Basic De-romanization Table

Basic Romaji					
Roman	A	I	U	E	O
Kana	あ	い	う	え	お
Roman	KA	KI	KU	KE	KO
Kana	か	き	く	け	こ
Roman	SA	SI	SU	SE	SO
Kana	さ	し	す	せ	そ
Roman	TA	TI	TU	TE	TO
Kana	た	ち	つ	て	と
Roman	NA	NI	NU	NE	NO
Kana	な	に	ぬ	ね	の
Roman	HA	HI	HU	HE	HO
Kana	は	ひ	ふ	へ	ほ
Roman	MA	MI	MU	ME	MO
Kana	ま	み	む	め	も
Roman	YA		YU	YE	YO
Kana	や		ゆ	いえ	よ
Roman	RA	RI	RU	RE	RO
Kana	ら	り	る	れ	ろ
Roman	WA	WI	WU	WE	WO
Kana	わ	うい	う	うえ	を
Voiced Consonants (Dakuon)					
Roman	GA	GI	GU	GE	GO
Kana	が	ぎ	ぐ	げ	ご
Roman	ZA	ZI	ZU	ZE	ZO
Kana	ざ	じ	ず	ぜ	ぞ
Roman	DA	DI	DU	DE	DO
Kana	だ	ぢ	づ	で	ど
Roman	BA	BI	BU	BE	BO
Kana	ば	び	ぶ	べ	ぼ
Unvoiced Consonants (Han-Dakuon)					
Roman	PA	PI	PU	PE	PO
Kana	ぱ	ぴ	ぷ	ぺ	ぽ
Unvoiced Consonants (Yo-on)					
Roman	FA	FI	FU	FE	FO
Kana	ふぁ	ふぃ	ふ	ふぇ	ふぉ
Roman	SHA	SHI	SHU	SHE	SHO
Kana	しゃ	し	しゅ	しぇ	しょ
Roman	CHA	CHI	CHU	CHE	CHO
Kana	ちゃ	ち	ちゅ	ちぇ	ちょ

Table 2: Alignment Exapmles for JnJk Task

Unit	Source	Target
Roman	SUZ:UKI	鈴:木
Kana	**SUZU:KI**	**鈴:木**
Roman	HIR:OMI	裕:実
Kana	**HIRO:MI**	**裕:実**
Roman	OK:UNO	奥:野
Kana	**OKU:NO**	**奥:野**
Roman	JU:NYA	順:也
Kana	**JUN:YA**	**順:也**

Table 3: Alignment Exapmles for EnJa Task

Unit	Source	Target
Char	J:u:s:mi:ne	ジ:ャ:ス:ミ:ン
Mora	**Ju:s:mi:ne**	**ジャ:ス:ミ:ン**
Char	C:h:a:p:li:n	チ:ャ:ッ:プ:リ:ン
Mora	**Cha:p:li:n**	**チャッ:プ:リ:ン**
Char	A:r:th:ur	ア:ー:サ:ー
Mora	**Ar:thur**	**アー:サー**

Table 4: Official Scores for 8 Language Pairs

Task	ACC	F-Score	MRR	MAP
ChEn	0.013	0.259	0.017	0.013
EnBa	0.404	0.882	0.515	0.403
EnCh	0.301	0.655	0.376	0.292
EnHe	0.191	0.808	0.254	0.190
EnJa	0.362	0.803	0.469	0.359
EnKo	0.334	0.688	0.411	0.334
EnPe	0.658	0.941	0.761	0.640
JnJk	0.512	0.693	0.582	0.401

5.2 Investigation for JnJk Task

We further investigated the results for JnJk task to compare baseline and proposed system.

Table 5 shows the results of JnJk task for development set. The settings of tools are determined by preliminary experiments. We used m2m-aligner with length limit of maxX == 6 and maxY == 1, mpaligner with no length limit, and DirecTL+ with context size 7 and n-gram order 1. Proposed system is combined with Japanese-specific heuristics including de-romanization.

The results show two facts; mpaligner greatly beats m2m-aligner, and proposed de-romanization improves more both baseline systems.

Table 5: Results on JnJk Task

Method	ACC	F-Score	MRR	MAP
m2m-aligner	0.113	0.389	0.182	0.114
mpaligner	0.121	0.391	0.197	0.122
Proposed	**0.199**	**0.494**	**0.300**	**0.200**

5.3 Investigation for EnJa Task

In this subsection, we show the results for EnJa task to compare baseline and proposed system.

Table 6 shows the results of EnJa task for development set. All of the settings of tools are set default in this investigation.

Again, mpaligner beats m2m-aligner and our mora-based alignment improves scores of baseline systems in this system.

Table 6: Results on EnJa Task

Method	ACC	F-Score	MRR	MAP
m2m-aligner	0.280	0.737	0.359	0.280
mpaligner	0.326	0.761	0.431	0.326
Proposed	**0.358**	**0.774**	**0.469**	**0.358**

6 Disccussion

We compared mpaligner and m2m-aligner in the framework of statistical machine transliteration. In Japanese language, mpaligner performs better than m2m-aligner. This fact shows that maximum likelihood estimation approach adopted by m2m-aligner is not suitable for the purpose of machine transliteration. More importantly in practice, mpaligner is free from hand-tuning for length limits.

We proposed two Japanese-specific heuristics, de-romanization for JnJk task and mora-based alignment for EnJa task. They are implemented as preprocessing for training data, and improved the results of transliteration by eliminating linguistically invalid alignments. This shows the possibility that character-based alignment may not be the best solution for machine transliteration.

Beside Japanese, there can be efficient heuristics for other languages. But, more interesting issue is whether we can find such heuristics automatically or not.

7 Conclusion

We applied mpaligner to machine transliteration task for the first time and we proposed Japanese-specific heuristics for JnJk and EnJa tasks.

We confirmed that the maximum likelihood estimation approach adopted by m2m-aligner performs poor for the purpose of machine transliteration. One of methods to cope with this issue is to penalize long alignment using mpaligner.

We proposed de-romanization for JnJk task, and mora-based alignment for EnJa task. In the experiments, they demonstrated their capability to improve accuracy greatly.

Our proposed heuristics are language-dependent while they can be combined with any other language-independent methods including (Finch et al., 2011) or (Hagiwara and Sekine, 2011).

For future work, language-dependent heuristics beside Japanese or methods to find such heuristics automatically should be developed.

Acknowledgments

References

Colin Cherry and Hisami Suzuki. 2009. Discriminative substring decoding for transliteration. In *Proceedings of the 2009 Conference on Empirical Methods in Natural Language Processing*, pages 1066–1075, Singapore, August. Association for Computational Linguistics.

Andrew Finch and Eiichiro Sumita. 2008. Phrase-based machine transliteration. In *Proceedings of the Workshop on Technologies and Corpora for Asia-Pacific*

Speech Translation (TCAST), pages 13–18, Hyderabad, India, January.

Andrew Finch and Eiichiro Sumita. 2010. A Bayesian Model of Bilingual Segmentation for Transliteration. In Marcello Federico, Ian Lane, Michael Paul, and François Yvon, editors, *Proceedings of the seventh International Workshop on Spoken Language Translation (IWSLT)*, pages 259–266.

Andrew Finch, Paul Dixon, and Eiichiro Sumita. 2011. Integrating models derived from non-parametric bayesian co-segmentation into a statistical machine transliteration system. In *Proceedings of the 3rd Named Entities Workshop (NEWS 2011)*, pages 23–27, Chiang Mai, Thailand, November. Asian Federation of Natural Language Processing.

Masato Hagiwara and Satoshi Sekine. 2011. Latent class transliteration based on source language origin. In *Proceedings of the 49th Annual Meeting of the Association for Computational Linguistics: Human Language Technologies*, pages 53–57, Portland, Oregon, USA, June. Association for Computational Linguistics.

Jun Hatori and Hisami Suzuki. 2011. Japanese pronunciation prediction as phrasal statistical machine translation. In *Proceedings of 5th International Joint Conference on Natural Language Processing*, pages 120–128, Chiang Mai, Thailand, November. Asian Federation of Natural Language Processing.

Sittichai Jiampojamarn, Grzegorz Kondrak, and Tarek Sherif. 2007. Applying many-to-many alignments and hidden markov models to letter-to-phoneme conversion. In *Human Language Technologies 2007: The Conference of the North American Chapter of the Association for Computational Linguistics; Proceedings of the Main Conference*, pages 372–379, Rochester, New York, April. Association for Computational Linguistics.

Sittichai Jiampojamarn, Colin Cherry, and Grzegorz Kondrak. 2008. Joint processing and discriminative training for letter-to-phoneme conversion. In *Proceedings of ACL-08: HLT*, pages 905–913, Columbus, Ohio, June. Association for Computational Linguistics.

Keigo Kubo, Hiromichi Kawanami, Hiroshi Saruwatari, and Kiyohiro Shikano. 2011. Unconstrained many-to-many alignment for automatic pronunciation annotation. In *Proceedings of Asia-Pacific Signal and Information Processing Association Annual Summit and Conference 2011 (APSIPA2011)*, Xi'an, China, October.

Min Zhang, A Kumaran, and Haizhou Li. 2012. Whitepaper of news 2012 shared task on machine transliteration. In *Proceedings of the 4th Named Entities Workshop (NEWS 2012)*, Jeju, Korea, July. The Association of Computational Linguistics.

Transliteration by Sequence Labeling with Lattice Encodings and Reranking

Waleed Ammar **Chris Dyer** **Noah A. Smith**
Language Technologies Institute
Carnegie Mellon University
Pittsburgh, PA, 15213, USA
{wammar,cdyer,nasmith}@cs.cmu.edu

Abstract

We consider the task of generating transliterated word forms. To allow for a wide range of interacting features, we use a conditional random field (CRF) sequence labeling model. We then present two innovations: a training objective that optimizes toward any of a set of possible correct labels (since more than one transliteration is often possible for a particular input), and a k-best reranking stage to incorporate nonlocal features. This paper presents results on the Arabic-English transliteration task of the NEWS 2012 workshop.

1 Introduction

Transliteration is the transformation of a piece of text from one language's writing system into another. Since the transformation is mostly explained as local substitutions, deletions, and insertions, we treat word transliteration as a **sequence labeling problem** (Ganesh et al., 2008; Reddy and Waxmonsky, 2009), using linear-chain conditional random fields as our model (Lafferty et al., 2001; Sha and Pereira, 2003). We tailor this model to the transliteration task in several ways.

First, for the Arabic-English task, each Arabic input is paired with multiple valid English transliteration outputs, any of which is judged to be correct. To effectively exploit these multiple references during learning, we use a training objective in which the model may favor some correct transliterations over the others. Computationally efficient inference is achieved by encoding the references in a lattice.

Second, inference for our first-order sequence labeling model requires a runtime that is quadratic in the number of labels. Since our labels are character n-grams in the target language, we must cope with thousands of labels. To make the most of each inference call during training, we apply a mini-batch training algorithm which converges quickly.

Finally, we wish to consider some global features that would render exact inference intractable. We therefore use a reranking model (Collins, 2000).

We demonstrate the performance benefits of these modifications on the Arabic-English transliteration task, using the open-source library `cdec` (Dyer et al., 2010)[1] for learning and prediction.

2 Problem Description

In the NEWS 2012 workshop, the task is to generate a list of ten transliterations in a specified target language for each named entity (in a known source language) in the test set. A training set is provided for each language pair. An entry in the training set comprises a named entity in the source language and one or more transliterations in the target language. Zhang et al. (2012) provides a detailed description of the shared task.

3 Approach

3.1 Character Alignment

In order to extract source-target character mappings, we use `m2m-aligner` (Jiampojamarn et al., 2007),[2] which implements a forward-backward algorithm to sum over probabilities of possible character sequence mappings, and uses Expectation Maximization to learn mapping probabilities. We allow source characters to be deleted, but not target characters. Parameters `-maxX` and `-maxY` are tuned on a devevelopment set.

Our running example is the Arabic name EAdl (in Buckwalter's ASCII-based encoding of Arabic) with two English transliterations: `ADEL` and `'ADIL`. The character alignment for the two pairs is shown in Fig. 1.

[1] http://www.cdec-decoder.org

[2] http://code.google.com/p/m2m-aligner

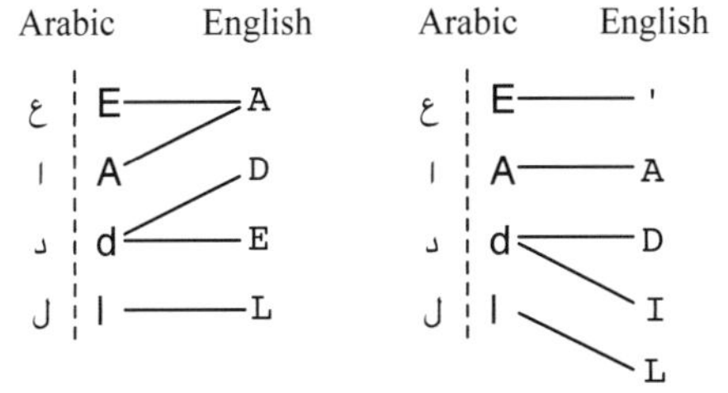

Figure 1: Character alignment for transliterating EAdl to ADEL and 'ADIL.

3.2 Sequence Labeling Scheme and Notation

We frame transliteration as a sequence labeling problem. However, transliteration is not a one-to-one process, meaning that a naïve application of one-label-per-token sequence models would be unlikely to perform well. Previous work has taken two different approaches. Reddy and Waxmonsky (2009) first segment the input character sequence, then use the segments to construct a transliteration in the target language. Since segmentation errors will compound to produce transliteration errors, we avoid this. Ganesh et al. (2008) do not require a segmentation step, but their model does not allow for many-to-one and many-to-many character mappings which are often necessary.

Our approach overcomes both these shortcomings: we have neither an explicit segmentation step, nor do we forbid many-to-many mappings. In our model, each character x_i in the source-language input $\mathbf{x} = \langle x_1, x_2, \ldots, x_n \rangle$ is assigned a label y_i. However, a label y_i is a *sequence* of one or more target-language characters, a special marker indicating a deletion (ϵ), or a special marker indicating involvement in a many-to-one mapping (δ), that is, $y_i \in \Sigma^+ \cup \{\epsilon, \delta\}$, where Σ is the target language alphabet.[3] When an input $\mathbf{x}$ has multiple alternative reference transliterations, we denote the set $\mathcal{Y}^*(\mathbf{x}) = \{\mathbf{y}^1, \mathbf{y}^2, \ldots, \mathbf{y}^K\}$.

We map the many-to-many alignments produced by `m2m-aligner` to one label for each input character, using the scheme in Table 1. Note that zero-to-one alignments are not allowed.

The two reference label sequences for our running example, which are constructed from the alignments in Fig. 1 are:

[3]For an input type x, we only consider labels that were actually observed in the training data, which means the label set is finite.

Type	Alignment	Labels
1:0	$x_i : \epsilon$	$y_i = \epsilon$
1:1	$x_i : t_j$	$y_i = t_j$
1:many	$x_i : t_j \ldots t_k$	$y_i = t_j \ldots t_k$
many:1	$x_i \ldots x_p : t_j$	$y_p = t_j$ $y_i = \cdots = y_{p-1} = \delta$
many:many	$x_i \ldots x_p : t_j \ldots t_k$	$y_p = t_j \ldots t_k$ $y_i = \cdots = y_{p-1} = \delta$

Table 1: Transforming alignments to sequence labels.

x	$\mathbf{y}^1$	$\mathbf{y}^2$
E	δ	'
A	A	A
d	DE	DI
l	L	L

Of key importance in our model is defining, for each source character, the set of labels that can be considered for it. For each source character, we add all labels consistent with character alignments to the lexicon.

3.3 Model

Our model for mapping from inputs to outputs is a conditional random field (Lafferty et al., 2001), which defines the conditional probability of every possible sequence labeling $\mathbf{y}$ of a sequence $\mathbf{x}$ with the parametric form:

$$p_{\boldsymbol{\lambda}}(\mathbf{y} \mid \mathbf{x}) \propto \exp \sum_{i=1}^{|\mathbf{x}|} \boldsymbol{\lambda} \cdot \mathbf{f}(\mathbf{x}, y_i, y_{i-1}) \quad (1)$$

where $\mathbf{f}$ is a vector of real-valued feature functions.

3.4 Features

The feature functions used are instantiated by applying templates shown in Table 2 to each position i in the input string $\mathbf{x}$.

3.5 Parameter Learning

Given a training dataset of pairs $\{\langle \mathbf{x}_j, \mathbf{y}_j \rangle\}_{j=1}^{\ell}$ (note that each $\mathbf{y}$ is derived from the max-scoring character alignment), a CRF is trained to maximize the regularized conditional log-likelihood:

$$\max_{\boldsymbol{\lambda}} \mathcal{L}_{\{1,\ldots,\ell\}}(\boldsymbol{\lambda}) \triangleq \sum_{j=1}^{\ell} \log p_{\boldsymbol{\lambda}}(\mathbf{y}_j \mid \mathbf{x}_j) - C\|\boldsymbol{\lambda}\|_2^2 \quad (2)$$

The regularization strength hyperparameter is tuned on development data. On account of the large data sizes and large label sets in several language pairs

Feature Template	Description
U1:y_i-x_i, U2:y_i-x_{i-1}-x_i, U3:y_i-x_i-x_{i+1}, U4:y_i-x_{i-2}-x_{i-1}-x_i, U5:y_i-x_{i-1}-x_i-x_{i+1}, U6:y_i-x_i-x_{i+1}-x_{i+2}	moving window of unigram, bigram and trigram context
U7:y_i, B1:y_i-y_{i-1}	label unigrams and bigrams
U8:$\|y_i\|$	label size (in characters)

Table 2: Feature templates for features extracted from transliteration hypotheses. The SMALLCAPS prefixes prevent accidental feature collisions.

(Table 3), batch optimization with L-BFGS is infeasible. Therefore, we use a variant of the mini-batch L-BFGS learning approach proposed by Le et al. (2011). This algorithm uses a series of randomly chosen mini-batches $\mathcal{B}^{(1)}, \mathcal{B}^{(2)}, \ldots$, each a subset of $\{1, \ldots, \ell\}$, to produce a series of weights $\boldsymbol{\lambda}^{(1)}, \boldsymbol{\lambda}^{(2)}, \ldots$ by running N iterations of L-BFGS on each mini-batch to compute the following:

$$\max_{\boldsymbol{\lambda}^{(i)}} \mathcal{L}_{\mathcal{B}^{(i)}}(\boldsymbol{\lambda}^{(i)}) - T\|\boldsymbol{\lambda}^{(i)} - \boldsymbol{\lambda}^{(i-1)}\|_2^2 \quad (3)$$

The T parameter controls how far from the previous weights the optimizer can move in any particular mini-batch[4]. We use mini-batch sizes of 5, and start training with a small value of T and increase it as we process more iterations. This is equivalent to reducing the step-size with the number of iterations in conventional stochastic learning algorithms.

Language Pair	Unique Labels
Arabic-English	1,240
Chinese-English	2,985
Thai-English	1,771
English-Chinese	1,321
English-Japanese Kanji	4,572

Table 3: Size of the label set in some language pairs.

3.6 Using Multiple Reference Transliterations

In some language pairs, NEWS-2012 provides multiple reference transliterations in the training set. In this section, we discuss two possibilities for using these multiple references to train our transliteration model. The first possibility is to create multiple independent training inputs for each input $\mathbf{x}$, one for each correct transliteration in $\mathcal{Y}^*(\mathbf{x})$. Using this approach, with K different transliterations, the CRF training objective will attempt to assign probability $\frac{1}{K}$ to each correct transliteration, and 0 to all others (modulo regularization).

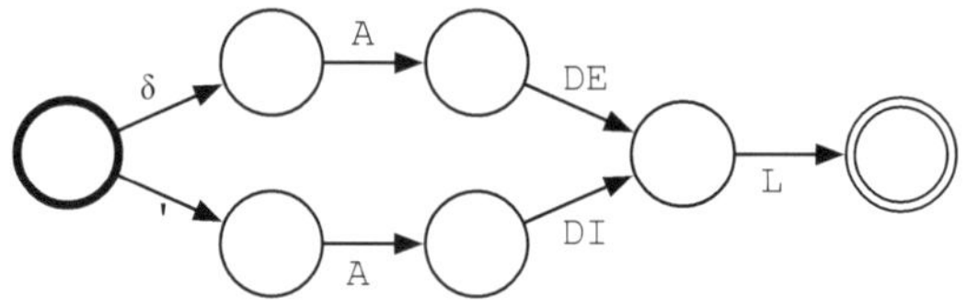

Figure 2: Lattice encoding two transliterations of EAdl: ADEL and 'ADIL.

Alternatively, we can train the model to maximize the *marginal* probability assigned by the model to the *set* of correct labels $\mathcal{Y}^* = \{\mathbf{y}^1, \ldots, \mathbf{y}^K\}$. That is, we assume a set of training data $\{(\mathbf{x}_j, \mathcal{Y}_j^*)\}_{j=1}^{\ell}$ and replace the standard CRF objective with the following (Dyer, 2009):[5]

$$\max_{\boldsymbol{\lambda}} \sum_{j=1}^{\ell} \log \sum_{\mathbf{y} \in \mathcal{Y}_j^*} p_{\boldsymbol{\lambda}}(\mathbf{y} \mid \mathbf{x}_j) - C\|\boldsymbol{\lambda}\|_2^2 \quad (4)$$

This learning objective has more flexibility. It can maximize the likelihood of the training data by giving uniform probability to each reference transliteration for a given $\mathbf{x}$, but it does not have to. In effect, we do not care how probability mass is distributed among the correct labels. Our hope is that if some transliterations are difficult to model—perhaps because they are incorrect—the model will be able to disregard them.

To calculate the marginal probability for each $\mathbf{x}_j$, we represent $\mathcal{Y}^*(\mathbf{x})$ as a *label lattice*, which is supported as label reference format in `cdec`. A further computational advantage is that each $\mathbf{x}$ in the training data is now only a single training instance meaning that fewer forward-backward evaluations are necessary. The lattice encoding of both transliterations of our running example is shown in Fig. 2.

3.7 Reranking

CRFs require feature functions to be "local" to cliques in the underlying graphical model. One way to incorporate global features is to first decode the

[4]When $T = 0$, our learning algorithm is identical to the L-BFGS mini-batch algorithm of Le et al. (2011); however, we find that more rapid convergence is possible when $T > 0$.

[5]Unlike the standard CRF objective in eq. 2, the marginal probability objective is non-convex, meaning that we are only guaranteed to converge to a local optimum in training.

k-best transliterations using the CRF, then rerank based on global features combined with the CRF's conditional probability of each candidate. We experiment with three non-local features:

Character language model: an estimate of $p_{charLM}(\mathbf{y})$ according to a trigram character language model (LM). While a bigram LM can be factored into local features in a first order CRF, higher n-gram orders require a higher-order CRF.

Class language model: an estimate of $p_{classLM}(\mathbf{y})$, similar to the character LM, but collapses characters which have a similar phonetic function into one class (vowels, consonants, and hyphens/spaces). Due to the reduced number of types in this model, we can train a 5-gram LM.

Transliteration length: an estimate of $p_{len}(|\mathbf{y}| \mid |\mathbf{x}|)$ assuming a multinomial distribution with parameters estimated using transliteration pairs of the training set.

The probabilistic model for each of the global features is trained using training data provided for the shared task. The reranking score is a linear combination of $\log p_{crf}(\mathbf{y} \mid \mathbf{x})$, $\log p_{charLM}(\mathbf{y})$, $\log p_{classLM}(\mathbf{y})$ and $\log p_{len}(|\mathbf{y}| \mid |\mathbf{x}|)$. Linear coefficients are optimized using simulated annealing, optimizing accuracy of the 1-best transliteration in a development set. k-best lists are extracted from the CRF trellis using the lazy enumeration algorithm of Huang and Chiang (2005).

4 Experiments

We tested on the NEWS 2012 Arabic-English dataset. The train, development, and test sets consist of 27,177, 1,292, and 1,296 source named entities, respectively, with an average 9.6 references per name in each case.

Table 4 summarizes our results using the ACC score (Zhang et al., 2012) (i.e., word accuracy in top-1). "Basic CRF" is the model with mini-batch learning and represents multiple reference transliterations as independent training examples. We manually tuned the number of training examples and LBFGS iterations per mini-batch to five and eight, respectively. "CRF w/lattice" compactly represents the multiple references in a lattice, as detailed in §3.6. We consider reranking using each of the three global features along with the CRF, as well as the full set of four features.

Model	Ar-En
Basic CRF	23.5
CRF w/lattice	37.0
CRF w/lattice; rerank p_{crf}, p_{charLM}	40.7
CRF w/lattice; rerank $p_{crf}, p_{classLM}$	38.4
CRF w/lattice; rerank p_{crf}, p_{len}	37.3
CRF w/lattice, rerank all four	**42.8**

Table 4: Model performance, measured in word accuracy in top-1 (ACC, %).

Maximizing the marginal conditional likelihood of the set of alternative transliterations (rather than maximizing each alternative independently) shows a dramatic improvement in transliteration accuracy for Arabic-English. Moreover, in Arabic-English the basic CRF model converges in 120K mini-batch iterations, which is, approximately, seven times the number of iterations needed for convergence with lattice-encoded labels. A model converges when its ACC score on the development set ceases to improve in 800 mini-batch iterations. Results also show that reranking a k-best list of only five transliterations with any of the global features improves accuracy. Using all the features together to rerank the k-best list gives further improvements.

5 Conclusion

We built a CRF transliteration model that allows for many-to-many character mappings. We address limitations of CRFs using mini-batch learning and reranking techniques. We also show how to relax the learning objective when the training set contains multiple references, resulting in faster convergence and improved transliteration accuracy.

We suspect that including features of higher-order n-gram labels would help improve transliteration accuracy further, but it makes inference intractable due to the large set of labels. In future work, coarse transformations of label n-grams might address this problem.

Acknowledgments

This research was supported in part by the U.S. Army Research Laboratory and the U.S. Army Research Office under contract/grant number W911NF-10-1-0533. We thank anonymous reviewers for the valuable comments.

References

M. Collins. 2000. Discriminative reranking for natural language parsing. In *Proc. of ICML*.

C. Dyer, A. Lopez, J. Ganitkevitch, J. Weese, F. Ture, P. Blunsom, H. Setiawan, V. Eidelman, and P. Resnik. 2010. cdec: A decoder, alignment, and learning framework for finite-state and context-free translation models. In *Proc. of ACL*.

C. Dyer. 2009. Using a maximum entropy model to build segmentation lattices for MT. In *Proc. of NAACL*.

S. Ganesh, S. Harsha, P. Pingali, and V. Varma. 2008. Statistical transliteration for cross language information retrieval using HMM alignment and CRF. In *Proc. of the 2nd Workshop On Cross Lingual Information Access*.

L. Huang and D. Chiang. 2005. Better k-best parsing. In *In Proc. of the 9th International Workshop on Parsing Technologies*.

S. Jiampojamarn, G. Kondrak, and T. Sherif. 2007. Applying many-to-many alignments and hidden Markov models to letter-to-phoneme conversion. In *Proc. of NAACL*.

J. Lafferty, A. McCallum, and F. Pereira. 2001. Conditional random fields: Probabilistic models for segmenting and labeling sequence data. In *Proc. of ICML*.

Q. V. Le, J. Ngiam, A. Coates, A. Lahiri, B. Prochnow, and A. Y. Ng. 2011. On optimization methods for deep learning. In *Proc. of ICML*.

S. Reddy and S. Waxmonsky. 2009. Substring-based transliteration with conditional random fields. In *Proc. of the Named Entities Workshop*.

F. Sha and F. Pereira. 2003. Shallow parsing with conditional random fields. In *Proc. of NAACL-HLT*.

M. Zhang, H. Li, M. Liu, and A. Kumaran. 2012. Whitepaper of NEWS 2012 shared task on machine transliteration.

Transliteration Experiments on Chinese and Arabic

Grzegorz Kondrak, Xingkai Li and **Mohammad Salameh**
Department of Computing Science
University of Alberta
Edmonton, AB, Canada, T6G 2E8
{gkondrak,xingkai,msalameh}@ualberta.ca

Abstract

We report the results of our transliteration experiments with language-specific adaptations in the context of two language pairs: English to Chinese, and Arabic to English. In particular, we investigate a syllable-based Pinyin intermediate representation for Chinese, and a letter mapping for Arabic.

1 Introduction

Transliteration transforms an orthographic form of a word in one writing script into an orthographic form of the same word in another writing script. The problem is challenging because the relationship between the source and target representations is often ambiguous. The process is further complicated by restrictions in the target phonological system.

DIRECTL+ (Jiampojamarn et al., 2010a) is an online discriminative training system that incorporates joint n-gram features and many-to-many alignments, which are generated by M2M-ALIGNER (Jiampojamarn et al., 2007). Our team employed variants of DIRECTL+ in the previous editions of the Shared Task on Transliteration (Jiampojamarn et al., 2009; Jiampojamarn et al., 2010b; Bhargava et al., 2011). Recently, Bhargava and Kondrak (2012) show significant improvement in accuracy for the English-to-Japanese task by leveraging supplemental transliterations from other scripts.

In this edition of the Shared Task on Transliteration, we experiment with language-specific adaptations for the EnCh and ArEn data sets. The structure of the paper is as follows. In Section 2, we provide details about the system parameters used in M2M-ALIGNER and DIRECTL+. Section 3 provides details of our strategies adopted in the EnCh task, which incorporate Chinese-specific knowledge and system combination algorithm. In Section 4 we elaborate on the difficulty of Arabic name transliteration and propose a letter mapping scheme. In Section 5 we present the official test results.

2 Base System

We run DIRECTL+ with all of the features described in (Jiampojamarn et al., 2010a). System parameters were determined during development. For the EnCh experiments, we set the context feature size to 5, the transition feature size to 2, and the joint n-gram feature size to 6. For the ArEn experiments, we used the same settings, except that we set the joint n-gram feature size to 5.

The M2M-ALIGNER parameters were set as follows. For the English-Pinyin alignment, the maximum substring length was 1 on the English side, and 2 on the Pinyin side, with empty substrings (*nulls*) allowed only on the Pinyin side. For ArEn, the maximum substring length was 2 for both sides.

3 English to Chinese

In this section, we introduce the strategies for improving DIRECTL+ performance on the EnCh task, including the use of Chinese Pinyin for preprocessing, and the combination of different models.

3.1 Data preprocessing and cleaning

In general, the preprocessing is limited to removing letter case distinctions in English names, and replacing every non-initial letter *x* with *ks*. However, we observed that the provided development set contains a number of entries (about 3%) that contain multiple English words on the source side, but no corresponding separators on the target side, whereas no such entries occur in the training or testing set. Since this discrepancy between sets may cause problems for alignment and generation, we separated the multi-word entries into individual words (using whitespace and apostrophes as delimiters) and manually selected proper transliteration targets for them. We also removed individual words that have no corresponding transliterations on the target side. The cleaned development set contains 2483 entries.

3.2 Alignment via Pinyin

Following Jiampojamarn et al. (2009; 2010b), we utilize Pinyin as an intermediate representation of Chinese characters during M2M alignment with the objective of improving its quality. Pinyin is the formally-adopted Romanization system for Standard Mandarin for the mapping of Chinese characters to Roman alphabet. It uses the 26 letters of the English alphabet except for the letter *v*, with the addition of the letter *ü*. Every Chinese character can be represented by a sequence of Pinyin letters according to the way it is pronounced. Numerous freely available online tools exist for facilitating Chinese-Pinyin conversion[1].

In our experiments, the original Chinese characters from the target side of the training set are converted to Pinyin before M2M alignment. A small part of them (about 50 out of approximately 500 distinct Chinese characters in the Shared Task data) have multiple pronunciations, and can thus be represented by different Pinyin sequences. For those characters we manually select the pronunciations that are normally used for names.

After the alignment between English and Pinyin representation has been generated by M2M-ALIGNER, we use it to derive the alignment between English and Chinese characters, which is then used for training DIRECTL+. This preprocessing step results in a more accurate alignment as it substantially reduces the number of target symbols from around 500 distinct Chinese characters to 26 Pinyin letters.

[1]For instance, `http://www.chinesetopinyin.com`

Our approach is to utilize Pinyin only in the alignment phase, and converts it back to Chinese characters before the training phase. We do not incorporate Pinyin into the generation phase in order to avoid problems involved in converting the transliteration results from Pinyin back to Chinese characters. For example, a Pinyin subsequence may have multiple Chinese character mappings because of the fact that many Chinese characters have the same Pinyin representation. In addition, it is not always clear how to partition the Pinyin sequence into substrings corresponding to individual Chinese characters.

The choice of the appropriate Chinese character sequence is the problem further complicating the conversion from Pinyin. We experimented with a trigram language model trained on the target Chinese side of the training set for the purpose of identifying the correct transliteration result. However, this approach yielded low accuracy on the development set. In contrast, the strategy of using Pinyin only for the alignment introduces no ambiguity because we know the mapping between Pinyin sequences and the target Chinese side of the training set.

3.3 Syllabic Pinyin

The Pinyin sequences representing the pronunciations of Chinese characters should not be interpreted as combinations of individual letters. Rather, a Mandarin phonetic syllable (the pronunciation of one Chinese character) is composed of an optional onset ("initial") followed by an obligatory rhyme ("final"). The rhyme itself is composed of an obligatory nucleus followed by an optional coda. Phonetically, the onset contains a single consonant, the nucleus contains a vowel or a diphthong, and the coda contains a single consonant ([r], [n] or [ŋ]). Both the onset and the rhyme can be represented by either a single letter or sequence of two or three letters. It is the initials and finals listed in Table 1 rather than Pinyin letters that are the phonemic units of Pinyin for Standard Mandarin. The pronunciation of a multi-letter initial/final is often different from the pronunciation of the sequence of its individual letters. Treating converted Pinyin as a sequence of separate letters may result in an incorrect phonetic transcription.

In this paper, we further experiment with encoding the converted sequences of Pinyin letters as the sequences of initials and finals for M2M alignment.

Initials							
b	p	m	f	d	t	n	l
g	k	h	j	q	x	zh	ch
sh	r	z	c	s	y	w	
Finals							
a	o	e	i	u	ü	ai	ei
ui	ao	ou	iu	ie	üe	er	an
en	in	un	ün	ang	eng	ing	ong

Table 1: The initials and finals in Chinese Pinyin.

Although the size of the alphabet increases from 26 letters to 47 initials and finals, the original Chinese pronunciation is represented more precisely. We refer to the new model which is trained on Pinyin initials and finals as PINYIN-SYL, and to the previously proposed model which is trained on Pinyin letters as PINYIN-LET.

3.4 System combination

The combination of models based on different principles may lead to improved prediction accuracy. We adopt the simple voting algorithm for system combination proposed by Jiampojamarn et al. (2009), with minor modifications. Since here we combine only two systems (PINYIN-LET and PINYIN-SYL), the algorithm becomes even simpler. We first rank the participating models according to their overall top-1 accuracy[2] on the development set. Note that the n-best list produced by DIRECTL+ may contain multiple copies of the same output which differ only in the implied input-output alignment. We allow such duplicates to contribute to the voting tally. The top-1 prediction is selected from the set of top-1 predictions produced by the participating models, with ties broken by voting and the preference for the highest-ranking system. For constructing n-best candidate lists, we order the candidate transliterations according to the highest rank assigned by either of the systems, with ties again broken by voting and the preference for the highest-ranking system. We refer to this combined model as COMBINED.

Table 2 shows the results of the three discussed approaches trained on the original training set, and tested on the cleaned development set. PINYIN-SYL performs slightly better than PINYIN-LET, which hints at the advantage of using Pinyin initials and finals over Pinyin letters as the intermediate representation during the alignment. The combination of the two models produces a marginally higher F-score[3]. The likely reason for the limited gain is the strong similarity of the two combined models. We experimented with adding a third model that is trained directly on the original Chinese characters without using Pinyin as the intermediate representation, but its accuracy was lower, and the accuracy of the resulting combined model was below PINYIN-SYL.

System	top-1	F-score
PINYIN-LET	0.296	0.679
PINYIN-SYL	0.302	0.681
COMBINED	0.304	0.682

Table 2: Development results on EnCh.

4 Arabic to English

Arabic script has 36 letters and 9 diacritics. Among these letters, the letters *Alif* and *Yaa* can be represented in different forms (أ آ إ ا and ي ى, respectively). The ArEn data set contains Arabic names without diacritics, which adds ambiguity to the transliteration task. When transliterated, such diacritics would appear as an English vowel. For example, it is difficult to tell whether the correct transliteration of the two-letter name بج is *Baj*, *Buj* or *Bij* because of the lacking vowel diacritic. Also, some Arabic consonants are transliterated into double English consonant because of the Shadda diacritic. Finally, some letters might have a different pronunciation (or none) when they occur at the end of the Arabic word. For example, the final letter ى is pronounced differently in أتمنى (*Atamana*) and بجانى (*Bagani*).

In the transliterations provided in the ArEn dataset, the different forms of *Alif*, the *Hamza* letter (ء), and the *Ain* letter (ع) are sometimes rendered as an apostrophe. In order to reduce the ambiguity, we devised a mapping shown in Table 3. The

[2]Word accuracy in top-1 evaluates only the top transliteration candidate produced by a transliteration system.

[3]The mean F-score measures how different, on average, the top transliteration candidate is from its closest reference.

Arabic	English
ا آ أ Alif forms, ة Taa Marbouta	a
ص Sahd, س Seen	s
ض Dahd, د Dal	d
ط Tah, ت Taa	t

Table 3: The mapping of Arabic letters to their English equivalents.

mapping reduces sets of Arabic letters that have the same corresponding English letter to a single higher-frequency symbol. For example, both ض and د characters tend to correspond to the letter d in English, so we replace all occurrences of the former with the latter. We refer to this variant as LETTER-MAP, as opposed to NO-MAP, which is the baseline system with no additional mapping.

Arabic compound names may be separated by space in their Arabic form or when transliterated. We treated the space similar to any alphabetic character. Also, any punctuation characters such as the apostrophe and hyphen on the English side are also treated as an alphabetic character.

System	top-1	F-score
NO-MAP	0.529	0.926
LETTER-MAP	0.519	0.925

Table 4: Development results on ArEn.

Table 4 shows our results on the original development set (2588 names). For these experiments, we split the original training set into a new training (25114 names) and development (2064 names) sets. The results indicate that the additional mapping actually decreases the overall accuracy with respect to the baseline. It seems that the mapping decreases the amount of information available to DIRECTL+, without sufficiently reducing the ambiguity. This confirms the previous findings that manually crafted rules for transliteration are generally ineffective (Karimi et al., 2011).

5 Final results

Table 5 shows our results as provided by the Shared Task organizers. For the EnCh task submission, we trained the PINYIN-LET and PINYIN-SYL models on the set that includes both the original training set and the cleaned development set. The output of the COMBINED system was designated as our Primary Run. The final results generally agree with our development results presented in Section 3, but the performance differences between models are smaller. For the ArEn task, we decided not to submit the output of the LETTER-MAP version because of the negative outcome of our development experiment.

Task	System	top-1	F-score
EnCh	PINYIN-LET	0.324	0.668
	PINYIN-SYL	0.325	0.673
	COMBINED	0.325	0.672
ArEn	NO-MAP	0.583	0.933

Table 5: Official test results.

According to the top-1 measure, our primary system was ranked second on the English-to-Chinese task, and third on the Arabic-to-English task. In both cases, we were within 0.5% of the best top-1 result. In addition, in both cases, we obtained the best results among the primary systems according to the F-score measure.

6 Conclusion

In this paper, we described our submission to the NEWS 2012 Shared Task on Machine Transliteration. In the EnCh task, our focus was on generating better alignment by employing Pinyin as the intermediate representation. A more coarse-grained representation that uses Pinyin initials and finals appears to be a step in the right direction. In the ArEn task, we found that reducing the number of distinct Arabic characters does not improve the accuracy of the base system.

Acknowledgments

We wish to thank Sittichai Jiampojamarn for help with DIRECTL+. This research was supported by the Natural Sciences and Engineering Research Council of Canada.

References

Aditya Bhargava and Grzegorz Kondrak. 2012. Leveraging supplemental representations for sequential transduction. In *Proceedings of the NAACL-HLT*.

Aditya Bhargava, Bradley Hauer, and Grzegorz Kondrak. 2011. Leveraging transliterations from multiple languages. In *Proceedings of the 3rd Named Entities Workshop (NEWS 2011)*, pages 36–40, Chiang Mai, Thailand, November. Asian Federation of Natural Language Processing.

Sittichai Jiampojamarn, Grzegorz Kondrak, and Tarek Sherif. 2007. Applying many-to-many alignments and hidden markov models to letter-to-phoneme conversion. In *Human Language Technologies 2007: The Conference of the North American Chapter of the Association for Computational Linguistics; Proceedings of the Main Conference*, pages 372–379, Rochester, New York, April. Association for Computational Linguistics.

Sittichai Jiampojamarn, Aditya Bhargava, Qing Dou, Kenneth Dwyer, and Grzegorz Kondrak. 2009. Directl: a language independent approach to transliteration. In *Proceedings of the 2009 Named Entities Workshop: Shared Task on Transliteration (NEWS 2009)*, pages 28–31, Suntec, Singapore, August. Association for Computational Linguistics.

Sittichai Jiampojamarn, Colin Cherry, and Grzegorz Kondrak. 2010a. Integrating joint n-gram features into a discriminative training framework. In *Human Language Technologies: The 2010 Annual Conference of the North American Chapter of the Association for Computational Linguistics*, pages 697–700, Los Angeles, California, June. Association for Computational Linguistics.

Sittichai Jiampojamarn, Kenneth Dwyer, Shane Bergsma, Aditya Bhargava, Qing Dou, Mi-Young Kim, and Grzegorz Kondrak. 2010b. Transliteration generation and mining with limited training resources. In *Proceedings of the 2010 Named Entities Workshop*, pages 39–47, Uppsala, Sweden, July. Association for Computational Linguistics.

Sarvnaz Karimi, Falk Scholer, and Andrew Turpin. 2011. Machine transliteration survey. *ACM Comput. Surv.*, 43(3):17:1–17:46, April.

Cost-benefit Analysis of Two-Stage Conditional Random Fields based English-to-Chinese Machine Transliteration

Chan-Hung Kuo[a] Shih-Hung Liu[ab] MikeTian-Jian Jiang[ac]
Cheng-Wei Lee[a] Wen-Lian Hsu[a]
[a]Institute of Information Science, Academia Sinica
[b]Department of Electrical Engineering, National Taiwan University
[c]Department of Computer Science, National Tsing Hua University
{laybow, journey, tmjiang, aska, hsu}@iis.sinica.edu.tw

Abstract

This work presents an English-to-Chinese (E2C) machine transliteration system based on two-stage conditional random fields (CRF) models with accessor variety (AV) as an additional feature to approximate local context of the source language. Experiment results show that two-stage CRF method outperforms the one-stage opponent since the former costs less to encode more features and finer grained labels than the latter.

1 Introduction

Machine transliteration is the phonetic transcription of names across languages and is essential in numerous natural language processing applications, such as machine translation, cross-language information retrieval/extraction, and automatic lexicon acquisition (Li et al., 2009). It can be either phoneme-based, grapheme-based, or a hybrid of the above. The phoneme-based approach transforms source and target names into comparable phonemes for an intuitive phonetic similarity measurement between two names (Knight and Graehl, 1998; Virga and Khudanpur, 2003). The grapheme-based approach, which treats transliteration as statistical machine translation problem under monotonic constraint, aims to obtain a direct orthographical mapping (DOM) to reduce possible errors introduced in multiple conversions (Li et al., 2004). The hybrid approach attempts to utilize both phoneme and grapheme information (Oh and Choi, 2006). Phoneme-based approaches are usually not good enough, because name entities have various etymological origins and transliterations are not always decided by pronunciations (Li et al., 2004). The state-of-the-art of transliteration approach is bilingual DOMs without intermediate phonetic projections (Yang et al., 2010).

Due to the success of CRF on sequential labeling problem (Lafferty et al., 2001), numerous machine transliteration systems applied it. Some of them treat transliteration as a two-stage sequential labeling problem: the first stage predicts syllable boundaries of source names, and the second stage uses those boundaries to get corresponding characters of target names (Yang et al., 2010; Qin and Chen, 2011). Dramatically de-creasing the cost of training with complex features is the major advantage of two-stage methods, but their downside is, compared to one-stage methods, features of target language are not directly applied in the first stage.

Richer context generally gains better results of sequential labeling, but squeezed performance always comes with a price of computational complexity. To balance cost and benefit for English-to-Chinese (E2C) transliteration, this work compares the one-stage method with the two-stage one, using additional features of AV (Feng et al., 2004) and M2M-aligner as an initial alignment (Jiampojamarn et al., 2007), to explore where the best investment reward is.

The remainder of this paper is organized as follows. Section 2 briefly introduces related works, including two-stage methods and AV. The machine transliteration system using M2M-aligner, CRF models, and AV features in this work is explained in Section 3. Section 4 describes experiment results along with a discussion in Section 5. Finally, Section 6 draws a conclusion.

2 Related Works

Reddy and Waxmonsky (2009) presented a phrase-based transliteration system that groups characters into substrings mapping onto target names, to demonstrate how a substring representation can be incorporated into CRF models with local context and phonemic information. Shishtla et al. (2009) adopted a statistical transliteration technique that consists of alignment models of GIZA++ (Och and Ney, 2003) and CRF models. Jiang et al. (2011) used M2M-aligner instead of GIZA++ and applied source grapheme's AV in a CRF-based transliteration.

A two-stage CRF-based transliteration was first designed to pipeline two independent processes (Yang et al., 2009). To recover from error propagations of the pipeline, a joint optimization of two-stage CRF method is then proposed to utilize n-best candidates of source name segmentations (Yang et al. 2010). Another approach to resist errors from the first stage is split training data into pools to lessen computation cost of sophisticated CRF models for the second stage (Qin and Chen, 2011).

3 System Description

3.1 EM for Initial Alignments

M2M-aligner first maximizes the probability of observed source-target pairs using EM algorithm and subsequently sets alignments via maximum *a posteriori* estimation. To obtain initial alignments as good as possible, this work empirically sets the parameter "maxX" of M2M-aligner for the maximum size of sub-alignments in the source side to 8, and sets the parameter "maxY" for the maximum size of sub-alignments in the target side to 1 (denoted as X8Y1 in short), since one of the well-known *a priori* of Chinese is that almost all Chinese characters are monosyllabic.

3.2 Format of Electronic Manuscript

The two-stage CRF method consists of syllable segmentation and Chinese character conversion CRF models, namely Stage-1 and Stage-2, respectively. Stage-1 CRF model is trained with source name segmentations initially aligned by M2M-aligner to predict syllable boundaries as accurate as possible. According to the discriminative power of CRF, some syllable boundary errors from preliminary alignments could be counterbalanced. Stage-2 CRF model then sees predicted syllable boundaries as input to produce optimal target names. For CRF modeling, this work uses Wapiti (Lavergne *et al.*, 2010).

Using "BULLOUGH" as an example, labeling schemes below are for Stage-1 training.

- B/*B* U/*B* L/*I* L/*I* O/*I* U/*I* G/*I* H/*E*
- B/*S* U/*B* L/*1* L/*2* O/*3* U/*4* G/*5* H/*E*

The first one is the common three-tag set "*BIE*". The last one is the eight-tag set "*B8*", including *B*, *1-5*, *E* and *S*: tag *B* indicates the beginning character of a syllable segment, tag *E* means the ending character, tag *I* or *1-5* stand for characters in-between, and tag *S* represents a single character segment. The expectation of the eight-tag set is the finer grained tags we used, the better segmentation accuracy we would gain.

For Stage-2, two labeling schemes are listed in the following.

- B/布 ULLOUGH/洛
- B/布 U/洛 L/*I* L/*I* O/*I* U/*I* G/*I* H/*I*

The former as substring-based labeling scheme are commonly used in two-stage CRF-based transliteration. Syllable segments in a source word are composed from Stage-1 results and then are associated with corresponding Chinese characters (Yang *et al.* 2009; Yang *et al.* 2010; Qin and Chen, 2011). The latter is a character-based labeling scheme where tags *B* or *S* from Stage-1 will be labeled with a Chinese character and others will be labeled as *I*. The merit of character-based method is to retrench the duration of the training, while substring-based method takes too much time to be included in this work for NEWS shared task. Section 5 will discuss more about pros and cons between substring and character based labeling schemes.

This work tests numerous CRF feature combinations, for example:

- C_{-3}, C_{-2}, C_{-1}, C_0, C_1, C_2, C_3 and
- $C_{-3}C_{-2}$, $C_{-2}C_{-1}$, $C_{-1}C_0$, C_0C_1, C_1C_2, C_2C_3,

where local context is ranging from -3 to 3, and C_i denotes the characters bound individually to the prediction label at its current position *i*.

3.3 CRF with AV

AV was for unsupervised Chinese word segmentation (Feng *et al.*, 2004). Jiang *et al.*, (2011) showed that using AV of source grapheme as CRF features could improve transliteration. In our two-stage system, Source AV is used in Stage-1 in hope for better syllable segmentations, but not in Stage-2 since it may be redundant and surely increase training cost of Stage-2.

4 Experiment Results

4.1 Results of Standard Runs

Four standard runs are submitted to NEWS12 E2C shared task. Their configurations are listed in Table 1, where "U" and "B" denote observation combinations of unigram and bigram, respectively. A digit in front of a "UB", for example, "2", indicates local context ranging from -2 to 2. P_{BIE} stands for "BIE" tag set and P_{B8} is for "B8" tag set. To summarize, the 4th (*i.e.* the primary) standard run exceeds 0.3 in terms of top-1 accuracy (ACC), and other ACCs of standard runs are approximate to 0.3. The 3rd standard run uses the one-stage CRF method to compare with the two-stage CRF method. Experiment results show that the two-stage CRF method can excel the one-stage opponent, while AV and richer context also improve performance.

ID	Configuration	ACC	Mean F-score
1	Two-stage, 2UB, P_{BIE}	0.295	0.652
2	Two-stage, 2UB, P_{BIE}, AV	0.299	0.659
3	One-stage, 3UB, P_{BIE}, AV	0.291	0.654
4	Two-stage, 3UB, P_{B8}, AV	0.311	0.662

Table 1. Selected E2C standard runs

ID	Configuration	ACC	Mean F-score
I	Two-stage, 2UB, P_{BIE}, AV	0.363	0.707
II	Two-stage, 3UB, P_{B8}, AV	0.397	0.727
III	One-stage, 3UB, P_{BIE}, AV	0.558	0.834

Table 2. Selected E2C inside tests

ID	Number of Features	Numbers of Label
II	Stage-1: 60,496 Stage-2: 2,567,618	Stage-1: 8 Stage-2: 547
III	4,439,896	548

Table 3. Cost of selected E2C inside tests

4.2 Results of Inside Tests

Numerous pilot tests have been conducted by training with both the training and development sets, and then testing on the development set, as "inside" tests. Three of them are shown in Table 2, where configurations I and II use the two-stage method, and configuration III is in one-stage. Table 2 suggests a trend that the one-stage CRF method performs better than the two-stage one on inside tests, but Table 1 votes the opposite. Since the development set includes semi-semantic transliterations that are unseen in both the training and the test sets (Jiang *et al.*, 2011), models of inside tests are probably over-fitted to these noises. Table 3 further indicates that the number of features in the one-stage CRF method is doubled than that in the two-stage one. By putting these observations together, the two-stage CRF method is believed to more effective and efficient than the one-stage CRF method.

5 Discussions

There are at least two major differences of two-stage CRF-based transliteration between our approach and others. One is that we enrich the local context as much as possible, such as using eight-tag set in Stage-1. The other is using a character-based labeling method instead of a substring-based one in Stage-2.

Reasonable alignments can cause CRF models troubles when a single source grapheme is mapped onto multiple phones. For instance, the alignment between "HAX" and "哈克斯" generating by M2M-aligner.

HA → 哈
X → 克斯

In this case, a single grapheme <X> pronounced as /ks/ in English therefore is associated with two Chinese characters "克斯", and won't be an easy case to common character-based linear-chain CRF. Although for the sake of efficiency, this work adopts character-based CRF models, only a few of such single grapheme for consonant blends or diphthongs appeared in training and test data, and then the decline of accuracy would be moderate. One may want to know how high the price is for using a substring-based method to solve this problem. We explore the number of features between substring-based and character-based

ID	Substring-based	Character-Based
II	106,070,874	2,567,618

Table 4. Number of features between substring and character based method in Stage-2

methods in Stage-2 with the same configuration II, as shown in Table 4. Features of substring-based method are tremendously more than character-based one. Qin (2011) also reported similar observations.

However, there is another issue in our character-based method: only the starting position of a source syllable segment will be labeled as Chinese character, others are labeled as *I*. Base on this labeling strategy, the local context of the target graphemes is missing.

6 Conclusions and Future Works

This work analyzes cost-benefit trade-offs between two-stage and one-stage CRF-based methods for E2C transliteration. Experiment results indicate that the two-stage method can outperform its one-stage opponent since the former costs less to encode more features and finer grained labels than the latter. Recommended future investigations would be encoding more features of target graphemes and utilizing *n*-best lattices from the outcome of Stage-1.

Acknowledgments

This research was supported in part by the National Science Council under grant NSC 100-2631-S-001-001, and the research center for Humanities and Social Sciences under grant IIS-50-23. The authors would like to thank anonymous reviewers for their constructive criticisms.

References

Haodi Feng, Kang Chen, Xiaotie Deng, and Wiemin Zheng. 2004. Accessor Variety Criteria for Chinese Word Extraction. *Computational Linguistics*, 30(1):75-93.

Zellig Sabbetai Harris. 1970. Morpheme boundaries within words. Papers in Structural and Transformational Linguistics, 68-77.

Sittichai Jiampojamarn, Grzegorz Kondrak and Tarek Sherif. 2007. Applying Many-to-Many Alignments and Hidden Markov Models to Letter-to-Phoneme Conversion. Proceedings of NAACL 2007, 372-379.

Mike Tian-Jian Jiang, Chan-Hung Kuo and Wen-Lian Hsu. 2011. English-to-Chinese Machine Transliteration using Accessor Variety Features of Source Graphemes. Proceedings of the 2011 Named Entities Workshop. 86-90.

K. Knight and J. Graehl. 1998. Machine Transliteration. Computational Linguistics, 24(4):599-612.

John Lafferty, Andrew McCallum, Fernando Pereira. 2001. Conditional Random Fields Probabilistic Models for Segmenting and Labeling Sequence Data. Proceedings of ICML, 591-598.

Thomas Lavergne, Oliver Cappé and François Yvon. 2010. Practical Very Large Scale CRF. Proceedings the 48th ACL, 504-513.

Haizhou Li, Min Zhang and Jian Su. 2004. A Joint Source Channel Model for Machine Transliteration. Proceedings of the 42nd ACL, 159-166.

Haizhou Li, A Kumaran, Min Zhang and Vladimir Pervouchine. 2009. Report of NEWS 2009 Transliteration Generation Shared Task. Proceedings of the 2009 Named Entities Workshop. 1-18.

Franz Josef Och and Hermann Ney. 2003. A Systematic Comparison of Various Statistical Alignment Models. Computational Linguistics, 29(1):19-51.

J. H. Oh and K. S. Choi. 2006. An Ensemble of Transliteration Models for Information Retrieval. Information Processing and Management, 42:980-1002.

Ying Qin. 2011. Phoneme strings based machine transliteration. Proceedings of the 7th IEEE International Conference on Natural Language Processing and Knowledge Engineering. 304-309.

Ying Qin and Guohua Chen. 2011. Forward-backward Machine Transliteration between English and Chinese Base on Combined CRF. Proceedings of the 2011 Named Entities Workshop. 82-85.

Eric Sven Ristad and Peter N. Yianilos. 1998. Learning String Edit Distance. IEEE Transactions on Pattern Recognition and Machine Intelligence, 20(5):522-532.

Sravana Reddy and Sonjia Waxmonsky. 2009. Substring-based transliteration with conditional random fields. Proceedings of the 2009 Named Entities Workshop, 92-95.

Praneeth Shishtla, V. Surya Ganesh, Sethuramalingam Subramaniam and Vasudeva Varma. 2009. A language-independent transliteration schema using character aligned models at NEWS 2009. Proceedings of the 2009 Named Entities Workshop, 40-43.

P. Virga and S. Khudanpur. 2003. Transliteration of Proper Names in Cross-lingual Information Retrieval. In the Proceedings of the ACL Workshop on Multilingual Named Entity Recognition.

Dong Yang, Paul Dixon, Yi-Cheng Pan, Tasuku Oonishi, Masanobu Nakamura, Sadaoki Furui. 2009. Combining a two-step conditional random field model and a joint source channel model for machine transliteration. Proceedings of the 2009 Named Entities Workshop, 72-75.

Dong Yang, Paul Dixon and Sadaoki Furui. 2010. Jointly optimizing a two-step conditional random field model for machine transliteration and its fast decoding algorithm. Proceedings of the ACL 2010. Conference Short Papers, 275-280

Hai Zhao and Chunyu Kit. 2008. Unsupervised Segmentation Helps Supervised Learning of Character Tagging for Word Segmentation and Named Entity Recognition. Proceedings of the Sixth SIGHAN Workshop on Chinese Language Processing.

Author Index